Become a Million-Dollar Property Developer:

An insider's guide to wealth, fulfilment, and glory.

JUSTIN GEHDE

Disclaimer
The information in this book is based on the author's personal experiences in completing property developments. The information provided is not financial advice, legal advice, town planning or other professional advice. If you intend to undertake a property development you should seek relevant advice for your particular circumstances. While reasonable care has been taken in producing this book, no guarantees are given in regard to the accuracy of its content or the material provided in any links. Any financial analysis in a case study, while illustrative of a property development, should not be considered average earnings, actual earnings or any promise or guarantee of future earnings.

Dedication

This book is dedicated to my wife Belinda and our two kids, and my mum and dad, Marie and Mike. Thank you for the unwavering support and an amazing life.

Table of Contents

1. Why I Wrote this Book

"Don't be afraid to give up the good to go for the great!"
John D. Rockefeller

"Congratulations, it's yours!" With those words from the selling agent, I started my first real property development project. It was my first property investment ever. I'd never bought a property before. The 48 hours prior were highly stressful while I waited to hear whether I secured the property or not. What would this 3,000 square metre site become? A lot more than I ever bargained for, as I'll explain.

What a rollercoaster ride it has been since that moment. If you told me in 2010 what would happen to me over the next 10 years, I would have laughed and called you crazy. Looking back, it has been a remarkable journey. I went from a public servant to a full-time property developer. If I can do it, you can too.

In this book, I will share how I succeeded in delivering a 20-townhouse project on my first property development project and what I learned along the way. Yes, you read that correctly, my first project was a 20-unit development that made well over $1 million. I will also go over how I went on to tackle two more 14-unit projects, lost an appeal at the planning court, and transformed my life along the way.

En-route, I started my own podcast called the Property Developer Podcast. Be sure to check it out at www.propertydeveloperpodcast.com if you haven't already. I also produced my signature online course called the Property Developer Training to help people tap into the wealth that property development can deliver, with less risk than you might think.

Head over to www.propertydevelopertraining.com to find out more about how the training can help you get started in property development.

In the following pages, you will find a secret code to secure an awesome discount on the training, so keep an eye out for it.

This is not really a nuts-and-bolts book about how to do a development project, that's what my training is for. However, I do cover important topics that you should be aware of if you are thinking of getting into property development. This book might be enough to whet your appetite and encourage you to take tangible steps toward getting into property development. It could be the ticket to transforming your life into one of wealth, fulfilment, and glory.

I will show you a pathway to generating a million dollars from low-risk projects in the span of five years. Imagine what an extra couple of hundred thousand dollars every few years could do for your wealth! You could be Australia's next million-dollar developer.

If you would like to see how ready you are to become a property developer, take my free short quiz at www.propertydevelopertraining.com/quiz

I hope this book provides you with some inspiration about how you can take control of your financial destiny through property development and build the life of your dreams.

2. Becoming a million-dollar developer

*"There is nothing sweeter than to dwell in towers that rise
on high, serene and fortified with teachings of the wise,
from which you may peer down upon others as they stray."*
Lucretius

How do you become a million-dollar developer? Is it when you develop a project worth more than a million dollars? I'd say no. Is it when you make a profit of more than a million dollars (before tax and profit sharing)? Yep, if you make the deal happen. Is it when you walk away with a million dollars in your pocket? Absolutely. Is it when you have a million dollars' worth of cash or equity from doing projects? You bet.

What I will show in this book is that earning a million dollars from property development is not as hard as you may think it is. In fact, you could be the next million-dollar property developer. For many people, property development is the quickest way to a million dollars.

For most people who earn a salary, I am sure this is true. There are few jobs or professions where you can earn a million dollars, in say five years, like you can in property development. Will it be easy? Nope. Will you enjoy it? Sure, if you are well suited for what's involved, which we will cover.

Even if you like your job and want to continue working, you can leverage property development to grow your wealth even faster. Dedicate an hour and a half a day to managing a small project and watch your wealth grow year after year.

The best part is that you can start right now by heading to www.propertydevelopertraining.com and doing my online course. It will take you step by step through the property development process. It will give you everything you need to know to start on your first small duplex or multi-unit development project. You can do the training in your own time and at your own pace.

I cover:

- the entire development cycle

- preparing for a project

- building your dream team (who will you need and when)

- how much cash will you need to complete your project

- finding a great development site

- preparing a fantastic planning application

- going through planning to get a planning permit

- pre construction activities including selling off the plan

- preparing construction documentation

- finding an awesome builder

- financial feasibilities and project funding essentials

- building contracts and the construction process

- completing the project and getting your profits.

Checklists and Guides

In the training, you will have access to stacks of checklists and guides to help you along the way, including important questions to ask potential team members before bringing them on board.

I consistently add bonus modules and content to the training, so it keeps getting better.

Head over to www.propertydevelopertraining.com and check out everything the training includes. Use the promo code 'book' to get a big fat discount. Do it now, and I will see you inside. Property development glory awaits.

3. My story - an unusual pathway to property development

"The more I learn, the more I realise how much I don't know."
Albert Einstein

Why should you be listening to me about becoming a million-dollar property developer? What have I done? What have I achieved? It's funny when I think back about my property development journey. It's been pretty interesting. I'm the first to admit I've made a lot of mistakes, some of them expensive - all of them repaired, and I've had an unusual pathway to property development.

In fact, I bought my first ever property in my mid-30s. My inaugural project was a development site which ended up being a 20-unit development. I had never actually invested in property before buying a development site. So how did I go from having zero property investments and no development experience to leading large multi-unit development projects?

My background is in corporate communication and public relations. I went to university, did a business degree in business communication, and worked in corporate roles for close to 18 years. I spent the last 12 of those years working in a public sector role. It was a good job and I enjoyed it, but I couldn't honestly say that I loved it. I know many people can relate with that notion.

Where my story differs is that I did something about finding a career I love and find fulfilling.

I think it's safe to say that I didn't have a conventional pathway into property development, and that's good news for you. There is no specific acceptable route into property ownership or into property developing. Even if you're in some obscure industry or you've never had any interaction or experience with property, you can still jump into property developing.

Even though it is not essential, most people that make their way into property development do seem to have some connection to the real estate industry. Either they've been investing in property, or they've worked in some sort of industry related to real estate. However, I am a shining example that you do not need to have any of those attributes or connections to be successful in property development.

Changing direction

How and why did I make the switch into property development? Well, when my first child was born, I had one of those periods in life- in my mid-thirties- where I started to reflect and contemplate about where I'd come from and where I wanted to go. I came to the realisation that I didn't want to do what I was doing for the rest of my life. I remember when I went to a professional development course, the leader of that program asked me about my career progression. They recommended looking up the line in terms of identifying what kind of position or career you aspire to have.

That was a good question because I looked up the line and thought, do I really want my manager's job? Not really. Do I want the job of the director of the business unit that I worked in? Again, not particularly. What about the executive director of the division? No, again. I didn't see myself in that kind of role. What about the head of the organisation? Is that a position that I would aspire to? I didn't aspire to any of those roles. I didn't really see a career pathway into any of those senior roles that excited and inspired me.

Then I started contemplating about what I would love to do. What would inspire me? What would I find fulfilling? I, like many people, had an interest in property. I loved watching television shows about people buying properties, property renovations, transformations of properties, etc. I was always really interested in them, but a word of warning to people out there; property development is nothing like what you see on any of those reality TV shows. It is far, far from it. So don't fall into the belief that full renovations take a weekend to complete and cost $15,000!

I started doing a lot of research into property, and my plan was to get into property investing. I started reading books about property investing. I read all the classic books that you're probably aware of. Steve McKnight's 0 to 130 properties. Jan Somers' books on property investing in Australia and many more. All those classic investment books and property investment resources. I was listening to a lot of podcasts about property investing, and it really got my juices flowing.

I formulated a strategy in my head but the one drawback that stopped me from taking the leap into property was the time that it would take for my investments to make significant returns and let me do what I wanted with my life. Isn't that why you invest in property? To one day live a life of freedom and choose what to do with your days?

The time frame involved in property investing was just too long for my personality and my risk profile. Waiting seven or eight years for a property to start having significant amounts of equity and positive cash flow was just too long for me. Slowly building up a base of properties and continuing to work to pay off their loans wasn't appealing to me either.

Property development lightbulb

One day, I was listening to a property investing podcast and there was a guest on the show talking about property development. The way he explained property development made sense to me and answered some questions about how you get into it. He provided insight into the fact that you didn't have to do everything yourself and that you could engage a team to do a lot of key tasks for you. That really resonated with me. I had one of those lightbulb moments where the realisation popped and I thought, that's it! That's what I want to do! I want to do property development.

I remember floating the idea of doing a property development course with my wife and explaining to her that it would be our ticket to freedom. Needless to say, she wasn't totally convinced. You can only imagine the response from my parents when I mentioned it to them too. It didn't matter because I was sold on the idea, and I was committed to making it work.

I enrolled in a mentoring program and started learning about property development. My intention was to do a three or four-unit townhouse project. The first area that I started searching for a site was the Melbourne bayside suburb of Frankston because it wasn't too far away from where I lived. At the time, it was an area that I could afford, and I could easily travel down to check out sites and meet with consultants.

The First Chapter

My search kicked off with all the vigour of an enthusiastic beginner, and after not too long, I came across a site right near the heart of Frankston that seemed perfect for the kind of project that I wanted to do. I managed to secure the site with a due diligence clause, and I thought I could get six units on this site because there was a similar sized property right next door. It had six small single level villas or units on it.

I'd been talking to a local draftsperson about helping me and I had secured the site without even making a deposit. In hindsight, this was quite an amazing feat. Although, it wasn't something I had negotiated. It was just that the agent never asked for any deposit.

I swung into action and instructed the draftsperson to prepare a plan for the site. I knew we needed to get six units on there and ordered a survey of the site, soil testing, and all the things I was taught to do during a due diligence period. It was exciting.

After a couple of weeks, the draftsperson came back with his plan, and this is where things started to go awry. Instead of just sketching up a simple scheme to confirm that we could have six units on the site, with rough sizes of what those properties would look like, he prepared a full-blown town planning drawing package.

He made detailed drawings ready for a town planning submission, which is a lot of detail and work. This was more than what I needed at this early stage of the project. He got six units on the site, but they weren't small, single level properties. They were all two-storey townhouses and, unfortunately, they were too big for what they would cost to build compared to what they would sell for when finished.

Getting it wrong

The proposed units were twice the size of the existing units next door. Based on that, I decided I needed to pull out of the deal because the project just wasn't going to work. It wasn't financially feasible to continue. After much consideration, I made the painful decision to withdraw from the contract.

Here is one good part of this story. I did have the due diligence clause and that allowed me to exit from the contract without penalty, and so I exercised that right.

However, the vendor of the property was not very happy about this because he was going through a divorce and really needed to sell the property so he could settle with his ex-wife. He was very grumpy that I had pulled out of the contract and somehow got a hold of my mobile number. He repeatedly called me and left nasty messages on my phone. That was a bit unsettling at the time.

There was still a big sting about walking away from that deal because it ended up costing me a lot of money in other areas. The design fees were about $5,000 because the draftsperson created a full design package without checking in with me. Instead of doing a simple plan with a sketch to gauge what we could include, he did a stack of work and drawings. In hindsight, this was my fault for not being clear enough in my brief and checking in after a few days to see how things were going.

With design fees and other costs like getting surveys, I saw about $8,000 of my hard-earned savings go down the drain. It was money spent for nothing but experience.

This hiccup really knocked me around. It took the wind out of my sails, and I was a bit dispirited for a while. It took me about nine months to pull myself together, get back into the game, and fully commit to doing a project. I felt foolish that I allowed this to happen.

Valuable lessons

I learned some valuable lessons from that episode. The first one is that you must be clear on what you expect from consultants in terms of their output and the price that you anticipate to pay for something. Also, don't go and blow your hard-earned savings on something that you are uncertain about. I was not clear and certain about what I was able to do or wanted to do on that site.

I was relying on the draftsperson to decide that for me and that was a mistake.

In property development, you need to have a clear idea about what you want to do on a site and if it is realistic before jumping into a deal. Once you figure out what you want to achieve, then you get your consultants to confirm your expectations. This brings me to the most important part of the lessons that I learned from the Frankston experience, and that is the importance of the due diligence clause and the need to use it very wisely.

So that was my first introduction to property development and it's fair to say that it didn't go particularly smoothly. I was not happy with myself for getting into that situation. Despite having all the help and support from the mentoring program, I still managed to go and blow a lot of money for no result.

After I picked myself up and dusted myself off, I was ready to get back in the game. Despite the setback I still really wanted to get into development. I didn't let this one stumble stop me from doing a project. I was still very committed to getting into property development.

The Second Coming

Fortunately, my second attempt at getting a project started was a lot better and far more interesting. With renewed vigour and determination I resumed my hunt for a project site, and decided to shift the area where I was prospecting to the outer suburbs of eastern Melbourne.

I was now looking for a larger site because I figured out that for the extra investment a five or a six-unit site was more profitable than a three or a four-unit site.

To do that, I needed a slightly bigger site than the 1,000 square metre lots I had been trying to find. I started looking around Croydon for a site that was about 1,600 square metres. I was confident I could do a profitable six-unit project on that sized block.

It was also at this stage that I realised that if I went a little bit bigger on the size of the site, it would stretch beyond my financial resources. So, I decided to see if I could bring in an investment partner to share the risk and reward. I approached a family member and asked them if they were interested in investing in the project. I prepared a proposal for them outlining what I was trying to do, the returns to expect, and the proposed arrangement for the deal.

I presented it to them. They were happy with the proposal and potential returns. We made a commercial agreement; it was put down on paper and we committed to the project. I got very busy searching for a site.

Finding the one

It was during this period when I was scouring for sites in Croydon that I came across a much larger site in the neighbouring suburb of Mooroolbark. This was a 3,000 square metre site, so nearly double in size to what I was looking for. It was a property that had passed-in at auction and was just sitting on the market.

This was during the Great Financial Crisis in 2013, so it was a really soft period of time in the property market. Nobody was interested in this large site primarily because it was covered in trees. That scared off a lot of people. But it was a terrific location, great size, and right near the centre of the town, so it screamed potential. It was on a main road, but it was set back with a big road reserve in between the road and the front of the property.

The property was advertised with a price guide that was only a little bit more than what we planned on paying for a site in Croydon. My budget at the time to buy a site in Croydon was around $650,000 and this larger site was on the market for $840,000 to $860,000. It makes my eyes water to write down those prices! Land prices in Melbourne have nearly tripled since then!

The property was a little bit more expensive than what we budgeted on spending, but we could get more units on it so the return on investment was going to be better. I figured that we could get 10 units on the site, all single level, which would be perfect for the local market. With plenty of people looking to move into smaller single-level dwellings, I thought it would be a great project.

I discussed with my partner whether we should go for it considering the benefits of going a little bit bigger. He agreed that we could stretch our budget and go for the bigger property. I started looking deeper at the site. I probably looked at that site for about two months because no one was interested in it.

The number of property transactions were pretty low back in 2013, and so I had lots of time to check out the site. This was a great benefit because there was a lot to consider.

I engaged a local draftsperson to help me with the project. I asked them to develop a simple sketch plan for a 10-unit site, which they duly did. It confirmed that we could comfortably fit the 10 townhouses on the block. Everything was looking pretty good.

In that period of time, I was also able to work out how I could deal with the trees on the site, which were a big issue as there were so many of them. But after a lot of investigation and discussion with an arborist I was able to work out how we could legally remove all but two trees off the site. Once I had figured that out, and the drafty confirmed we could fit 10 units on the site, the project became viable. The hairs on the back of my neck were bristling with excitement.

Securing the site

I got to a point where I was feeling pretty comfortable about making an offer. I had been in constant contact with the agent, and we had discussed including things like a due diligence clause in my offer and of course the amount we were prepared to pay.

I was able to ascertain from the agent that it was a deceased estate and there were four children who were selling the property. They were open to offers but at a minimum they wanted $800,000. Since the market was pretty slow, and no one else was interested, I thought I could offer them $760,000. I made a formal offer of $760,000, even though that was probably a bit too low even in a soft market. However, I was naive in thinking that they would accept it.

Sadly, they knocked back the offer. Then a funny thing happened. A second person entered into the picture and created competition. The agent had managed to get somebody else interested in the site. Now I was in a bidding war.

I was in the situation where I had to make a new and final offer. I had to decide what my best offer was going to be. I didn't want to lose the site; I knew it was a winner. In the end, I decided to put in an offer of $800,000 with a due diligence clause of 14 business days. I didn't really need the due diligence clause at this stage as I'd pretty much worked everything out by then. I was confident it was all going to work, but I wanted that extra safety net just in case.

I submitted my offer of $800,000 and then nervously sat back and waited to find out if the offer was going to be accepted. I can tell you that the next 24 hours was probably one of the most stressful periods of my life. My heart rate was up. My blood pressure was up. I was anxiously waiting to hear about whether or not the offer had been accepted.

Then finally, after what seemed like forever, the good news came. My offer had been accepted. This was fantastic news and I was very excited about securing the site.

The successful offer

Years later, I met the guy who I competed against, and we have since become friendly colleagues. I also discovered later that the only reason my offer was accepted instead of his was because I had more simple terms. He had offered a similar amount of money, in fact the same amount, but he had some conditions that were more onerous than what I had offered. The vendors had opted to take my offer, which I was very glad about.

Another interesting point to note here is that the agent later informed me that one of the key reasons that the vendors wanted $800,000 was because there were four siblings, and they wanted a nice round number that they could evenly divide among themselves. That was one of the reasons they didn't like the offer of $760,000. They wanted $800,000 so that they would each get $200,000.

This is something to keep in mind when you're making offers for properties. Sometimes there's a reason why the vendors want a particular price. There may be multiple people involved in the deal, and they may want a certain amount each. It's always good to try to understand and determine who the vendors are and what their motivations are.

I had secured my first site and I was feeling excited about it. I'd done a lot of due diligence. I'd looked at all the properties on the market in the area and what they'd sold for. I was very confident in my numbers.

It was time to really get the ball rolling and formally initiate the work on the town planning application for the 10 units.

A funny thing happened

It took about three months to fully prepare the drawings and reports for the town planning application. Once they were ready, we submitted our package to the local council. Then a funny thing happened. The council came back to us to say they had reviewed our design proposal and wanted to see more dwellings on the property. They felt the site was being underdeveloped.

Now this is something that's very rare in property development. Councils hardly ever ask for more units to be added to a project. However, the council had recently changed some of the planning rules in the area and were looking to encourage more development in certain parts of the suburb. This site happened to be within one of those areas where they wanted more development. Because it was a new policy change, and my site was so large, the council was looking to aggressively implement the policy intent of the new zoning change with our application.

The Council was pushing for higher density in the areas around local townships, which is where our property was located. They came back and said that they wanted to see more intense development of the site, including some terrace style properties.

I was scratching my head thinking this is a bit weird that council wants us to put more units on the site. I instructed the drafty to revise the design and we came up with a 14-townhouse proposal with a mixture of double and single storey townhouses. We included four terrace style dwellings across the front.

We resubmitted the application and I thought we had nailed it. Lo and behold, the council once again came back and said they still want to see more dwellings. In fact, they wanted to see at least another three to five units on the site!

You can imagine what I'm thinking at this point in time! I started off looking to do a six-unit development in Croydon, and now I'm looking at doing a 17 to 19 townhouse development in Mooroolbark. WTF.

Tripling the yield

You might be thinking, well, that's fantastic, you've tripled the yield that you're looking to get on the project, and yes, that's true. But everything else triples along with it. The amount of cash that you need to invest, the risk that you're taking on, the time frame extends beyond what you thought, and everything else just gets bigger. For a guy doing his first development, this was a big change and created a lot of questions. Could I do this? Can I manage such a big project to completion?

Now, fortunately, my business partner was happy to roll with the punches. We were happy to take on the extra risk and additional financial investment.

It was also at this stage that I realised I needed a new team working on the project. The local drafty was not the right person to get me through this, so I let them go. I engaged a young architect who had been recommended to me by someone I knew who had a lot of experience in property development. I spoke to the architect, called Dom, and I liked what he had to say.

Dom offered to prepare a scheme for the site that he thought would appeal to council. He came up with a new design of 20 townhouses. There was a row of 10 townhouses at the back and a row of 10 townhouses at the front with an L-shaped driveway coming from the left edge of the property and then through the middle of the site so that all the garages would be accessed from the internal driveway. It was a remarkable sight, seeing 20 units on the block. I decided to appoint Dom to work on the project.

We presented the concept to the council, and they were very supportive of it. From there, things started to really gather momentum. Up until that point, I just felt like we weren't really getting anywhere. It felt like running uphill all the time. But once we had the support of the council, there was a distinct change in the energy and momentum of the project.

Momentum is a funny, intangible element that is very important in a property development project because you want to keep things moving along, not get bogged down and become stagnant.

Gathering momentum

From there, things really felt like they started rolling downhill. We took the application to the public notice stage, only got three or four minor objections, and council proceeded to approve our application. I then moved to get the construction drawings done, engaged a local agent to help sell the product off the plan, and started moving towards construction.

At this stage, the Melbourne property market had really started to pick up from the GFC slump. This was in 2015, so the market was improving and making off the plan sales was becoming much easier than in the past couple of years. I can remember during the sales campaign when prices were jumping up by around $5,000 a month. We'd sell a unit at say $375,000 and the next month the same unit would easily get $380,000. It was incredible.

We were doing a pretty good job with our off the plan sales. We needed about 14 sales to meet the funding requirements of the bank we were talking with. Fourteen sales would roughly cover the cost of the construction loan, an essential hurdle for the bank funding. I will discuss this further in chapter 10 on construction funding basics.

While the sales were going on in the background, I worked on the construction costs and this was where I hit another snag. Along the way, I had been in regular discussions with a local builder about the project and he had been giving me rough construction estimates that he thought would cover the build cost based on the town planning drawings that I showed him.

I had a figure in my mind about what it was going to cost to build this project. Then, once I had all the construction documentation ready, I put the project out to tender. Imagine my surprise when the build quotes from the builder with whom I had been talking to came in about $400,000 higher than what we discussed.

Higher build costs

This was a shock to me and another period where I spent a lot of time trying to work out how to get the costs down. I probably lost three or four months scrambling around, trying to cut costs and reduce the build price. In the end, I opted to go with another local builder who tendered for the work and came in significantly cheaper than the original builder I planned on using.

I had to bite the bullet and sign up to a build price that was about $250,000 more than what I had budgeted for. However, there's a silver lining in this story. Fortunately, the booming property market helped to cover, and more than compensate, for the rising costs of construction. That was a win.

To cut short the rest of the story, I ended up building and delivering that 20-townhouse project. There were issues along the way, but we sold all the stock before it was finished. Everything settled without any real drama and the project made a lot of money. We banked well in excess of a million dollars in profit. I can still remember the day after all the settlements happened and there, sitting in the project bank account, was an amount that had six zeros in it. That was a pretty exciting day. I had landed the plane!

That was my first development, a little old 20-townhouse project. I learnt a lot, enjoyed it immensely, and was keen to go again.

Part Three - Taking it to the next level

Part three of this story is my next development. This is another tale of things not going according to plan.

While we were approaching the completion of the first project, I decided it was time to start another project because I felt confident that we could do it again. I started looking around for possible blocks of land and came across another good-looking site that was listed for sale in the neighbouring suburb. It was actually two blocks of land being sold together: a large battle axe block at the rear and the smaller parcel at the front. Together, they made up a roughly 3,000 square metre block approximately 30 metres across the front and 100 metres deep. It was similar in size to my other project. It had the same zoning and overlays and I thought this is another fantastic prospect.

I thought we could probably get a similar number of townhouses on that site as the project that had 20. I spoke with my team and got Dom to draw up a plan. Dom came up with a couple of different configurations before I settled on a 19-townhouse scheme.

I put together an investment proposal for that project and found some people prepared to invest and proceeded to secure that site, thinking this is going to be a slam dunk! We would get a permit pretty easily for this project because the council was so focused on encouraging a higher density outcome on these larger sites.

Based on that, I thought let's just go straight in with the 19 units, as that should be what the council wants.

We shouldn't have any issues.

Well, nothing could be further from the truth. Here is one of the big differences between the new site and the previous site. The previous site didn't really have any neighbours surrounding it. We only had three or four objections from people when we had the public notice period for the planning application.

However, the new site had about 20 neighbours abutting the site, including a retirement village. They were not happy about my shiny new 19-townhouse proposal.

Local resistance

The locals caused a lot of problems by all ganging up together and objecting to the proposal. They made life very difficult for the local councillor and they even appeared in an article in the local paper. All standing together out the front of the site looking grumpy. Now, for anyone who has any understanding about politics, politicians do not like being unpopular.

When lots of local people band together and let politicians know that they're not happy, they generally stand with the people. Especially against a supposedly big, bad developer. That's what happened to me. The 19-townhouse proposal ended up going to a council meeting for a vote instead of being approved by the planning department.

Interestingly, the planning report that was prepared for the councillors ahead of the council meeting indicated that we should get a permit for 17 townhouses, not the 19 townhouses we had proposed. The council's own planning officer felt that a 17-townhouse outcome would have been acceptable for the site, so that was encouraging.

However, at the council meeting, a lot of locals turned up. Some people carried placards and waved them around. Fortunately, there was no one there with an effigy of me, ready to set it alight, but the locals certainly made their position clear. They didn't want any development in their street.

Of course, the councillors voted to refuse our planning application. This was a disappointing and frustrating moment. I felt like we had ticked all the boxes in terms of providing a quality design and meeting all the planning guidelines.

We had two choices to make. Either accept the refusal and try again with a new application or take our application to the Victorian planning court/tribunal, which is called VCAT, and ask for the decision to be reviewed. You only get one shot at going to the planning tribunal, so you have to give it everything you have. At this stage, I was still very confident that we would get support from the tribunal for our application.

See you in court

I didn't want to take any chances. We engaged a specialist property barrister to represent us at the tribunal. We engaged an independent planning consultant to review our plans and provide expert evidence to the tribunal. We engaged a new landscaping consultant to prepare a completely new landscape plan and appear as an expert consultant at the tribunal (this was a guy who was meant to be amazing but didn't even use the right plants from the council's plant list in his new design... an embarrassing oversight that was highlighted when he appeared as a witness).

I can remember sitting at the hearing listening to the council put forward their side of the story and I can remember watching the body language of the tribunal member (judge) who was handling the case and thinking she's not really buying what we're putting down. I was worried.

Once the council had wrapped up their presentations our team put forward our side of the story.

We had principally stuck to our 19-townhouse scheme. We'd made a few modifications to it but we kept the principal design and layout that we had presented to council. We argued that the area was designated by the council through the planning rules for more intense development and that we were abiding by the intent of those rules, even if the locals didn't like it.

To cut a long and costly story short, sadly for us, the tribunal upheld the council's refusal and we lost.

We spent a lot of money and time trying to win and we didn't. You can imagine how disappointing it is to invest 18 months of time, effort, and money into a project only for it to be refused. In fact, it was closer to two years by the time we got a decision, with all the time the council had taken to assess the application, for it to be refused, for us to get our hearing at the tribunal, and for the decision to be handed down, before we reached that junction.

We were basically back at square one with some big decisions to make.

Confirmation bias

A big lesson for me that came out of this trip to the tribunal was the issue of confirmation bias. Everybody in our team was very confident that we would get approval for our application from the tribunal. They felt that we checked enough of the boxes to get the support of the tribunal and have the rejection overturned. What I was advised and told by members of the team aligned with my own belief and thinking, so I felt even more confident we would win.

As a property developer you are the captain of the team and must accept the results of the decisions you make. There is very little to be gained from blaming the members of your team. You hire them to provide their best advice but in the end, you have to make the call on what to do.

In hindsight, I think if we had made some modifications to the design and amended it to 17 townhouses like the planning officer's report had suggested, we might have got a different outcome, but we will never know.

After licking my wounds and reflecting on where we went wrong, I had to decide what we were going to do. I still felt strongly that this was a fantastic development site, which it was. It was really well located. It was a nice big block.

It enjoyed favourable zoning. It had a lot going for it. It had significant intrinsic value.

Fortunately, over the two years we had been tied up trying to get a permit, the property market had picked up a little bit and values were continuing to increase so the land was worth more and prices for new stock were rising. I decided to have another crack at the planning application and to modify our scheme down to 16 townhouses.

The team went back to work, and we submitted our proposal for 16 townhouses, got the same level of resistance from the local objectors, and to cut a long story short, we ended up negotiating on the design outcome and settled on a 14-townhouse scheme for which we finally received our permit.

Market fluctuation

Then a funny thing happened. The property market changed and started to soften and so getting our presales became pretty challenging.

It was much harder this time around to secure those off the plan sales than it was on the previous project. Again, we had the situation where the build costs ended up coming in much higher than expected.

This was a frustrating period of time for me because I was facing a softening property market, rising build costs, and the delays in the project we're adding significant blowouts to how long it was going to take to finish and get our money out of the project.

This was not part of the plan. The plan was to have projects finishing every year to help with cash flow and recycling capital. In fact, it had been so long between me getting paid for the first project and the likelihood of getting any significant money back from this project, that I actually had to go back into the workforce. I took a short-term, full-time contract to bring some money in.

Back on the project front, I had the dual challenges of rising construction costs and softening sales prices. It became apparent that we would never meet our pre-sales targets for bank funding in any period of time that would make the project viable.

At this point, we looked for a different funding solution than traditional bank funding and ended up going with a private fund that we had some connections with. The funding was more expensive, but it was more flexible in that we needed less pre-sales (only three sales this time). This meant we were able to get started much faster.

To add one more problem to the pile, after I had agreed to the construction price for the new development, which was already much higher than what I wanted it to be but had agreed to sign up for that price so we could get moving, the builder then repriced the project following industry price rises and the costs went up again by another $50,000. To say I was dismayed is an understatement!

Essentially, I was getting the same product for more money which was pretty frustrating to have to deal with. Once again, I bit the bullet and signed up to get the project rolling, with the view that we could continue to pick up sales at higher prices as the project unfolded.

Pandemic mayhem

After years of toil and challenge, we were ready to get started and everything was in place. The project took yet another twist as we got hit by the start of the COVID-19 pandemic beginning around March 2020.

There was so much uncertainty rolling across Australia about what would happen to the economy and the property markets. Fear was pervasive. I remember having a phone call with the lender where they said "what do you want to do with the project? Keep going or pause?" I couldn't see much benefit in pausing because we wanted to push ahead. So that's what we did and to the lender's credit, they supported our decision.

Construction finally got started in the middle of 2020. It was a minefield during the construction period as Melbourne entered a long and painful lockdown through the winter of 2020. There were periods when the number of people allowed on construction sites was limited and this affected our construction program. However, for the most part, work was able to continue.

Then another twist happened. This one for the better. In mid-2020, the federal government announced it was introducing measures to support and encourage the housing industry. They launched the Homebuilder Program to provide $25,000 grants to buyers of new property which led to a massive increase in demand from buyers. That increase in demand and heightened sales potential led to a subsequent sharp rise in prices. This was having a material impact on the project's bottom line. Things were finally starting to look better.

Market movements

We started to see a dramatic increase in buyer enquiry and that translated into sales. The increase in demand led to a reduction in stock across the market which resulted in rising prices. We started making quite a few sales at prices higher than I anticipated. In fact, by the time the project reached practical completion we only had one townhouse remaining for sale.

I had always planned on keeping that property until the end anyway as it was a standalone three-bedroom home with street frontage. I thought it would sell for a higher price when finished than what it would get if sold off the plan.

When construction wrapped up, I sold that final property at the end of 2021 at a price that made it worthwhile to hold onto until it was completed.

By the time we had finished construction, the project had ended up taking close to five years and cost a lot more in finance costs than originally intended. But we made more from our sales than we expected and everything worked out pretty well in the end. It certainly didn't go to plan, and I will always be grateful to the investors on the project for sticking it out and supporting me to the end, they were amazing.

I am really proud of that project and how it turned out. It is a fantastic looking development and I believe that it improves the design fabric of the local area. It is also a testament to determination and seeing something through to the end.

If you would like to hear more about what I took away from that crazy project, I shared some of the key lessons I learnt in episode 85 of the Property Developer Podcast
(listen at www.propertydeveloperpodcast.com).

Fourth Time Lucky

Part four of my development story was the acquisition of the block of land right next door to my first project. This was a 2,000 sqm block of land that I had my eye on from the start of the first project, as I could see it was another awesome block with great development potential.

My plan was to put 16 townhouses on the block, but as you can guess by now, things didn't go as smoothly as expected. However, I thought it would be smooth sailing, given that we had developed the site next door and council had pushed us to put the 20 townhouses on there. I figured that if we did something similar next door it would cruise through planning.

Sadly, it was not to be. The council had since changed their tune on what they wanted in these particular areas now. They weren't supportive of the level of density that they once had been pushing for. Now they were looking for things to be at the lower end of the density spectrum.

Once again, we went through a long drawn-out planning application period with council as we tried to get a permit for the 16 townhouses.

Here we go again

I couldn't understand how the council could not support what we proposed on the site considering how hard they pushed us next door but that's the fickle nature of council planning decisions sometimes.

There was a point in time toward the end of the planning process where I actually didn't know whether or not we would get approval from council or if we would have to go back to the planning tribunal. We were getting so much flak from the council about all sorts of strange things. They were just making it hard and difficult for us.

At one point the council tried to cancel our planning application saying we had missed a deadline for submitting a response to a request for further information. We argued back and forth with them pointing out that we did in fact submit a request for extension within the allowable time frame. This is where I learnt a little about the Interpretation of Legislation Act 1984 which provides definitions on how times and dates are defined in legislation in Victoria. Council stuck to their position, saying our application had lapsed and refusing to grant us an extension until a funny thing happened.

In the original letter the council sent us asking for a response to their queries, the council had inadvertently put the wrong year in the date by which we had to respond. The letter indicated we had to respond by 28 January 2018, which was actually the year before. It should have read 28 January 2019.

After weeks of saying our application had lapsed, the council magically granted us an extension of time once they realised their error. So by a small stroke of poor administration we managed to keep the application alive.

Again, to cut a long story short, I ended up negotiating an outcome for 14 townhouses. The council wanted to see more breaks in the built form and more ground floor living rather than reverse living areas (on the first floor) so we reduced the design by two units and opened up the development.

COVID strikes again

I got the permit for that project at the end of 2019 and was all set to get things underway in 2020 when COVID hit. The biggest spanner in the works with all the COVID chaos was that a moratorium on evictions came into effect in March 2020 just before I was about to ask the tenants in the house on the site to vacate. This meant we would have to wait until the end of March 2021 to issue a notice to vacate. So basically, we lost a year in the project because we couldn't demolish the house and get started on construction.

It did mean we could take our time getting our construction documentation done and select a builder for the project. But a funny thing happened during that period. Due to the surge in demand generated by the Homebuilder Program, new build numbers started going through the roof (pardon the pun) and a shortage of materials and labour, coupled with ongoing restrictions on the number of people who could work on building sites, started affecting the cost of construction.

In fact, construction costs started rising very rapidly. It was ridiculous. We agreed to a price with our selected builder in January 2021 and by April, when we were trying to finalise the contract price, the builder had to raise the price again due to industry cost increases.

I swallowed this again in order to keep things moving as I knew prices were going up quickly. However, there were still two more stings to come. In June, when we were about to sign the construction contract, the builder was forced to raise the price again due to more cost increases. We had seen a six percent price increase in six months. It was pretty hefty.

After I thought we had put the construction price issue to bed and right before building was due to start at the end of 2021, the builder came back again and said they needed an extra $200,000 or they would lose money and simply not start the project. This was a pretty surprising scenario to be in.

Pragmatism wins the day

In the end, the delays of finding a new builder meant it was more practical to negotiate a higher build cost and get things started. It was another lesson in having to be flexible and adaptable when working on a development project.

Fortunately, a lack of stock across the market, low interest rates, and pent-up demand from ongoing lockdowns meant property prices continued to rise as we started construction. So, we expect to make up the difference from increased sale prices.

At the time of writing, we have started construction and there's plenty of action on site. I am looking forward to bringing this project to the market and presenting another awesome development to prospective buyers.

That's a brief overview of my journey into property development. As you can see, it's been a bit of a roller coaster. I haven't really had any easy projects and that's meant that I've learnt a hell of a lot of lessons, many of which I've shared in this book and applied in the Property Developer Training.

If you want to get a bit of a taste of my projects and see what they look like, then head over to www.gehde.com.au

4. Why property development can be a good wealth strategy

"Great people plant trees they'll never sit under."
Alfred Whitehead

Let's look at why I like property development and why I think it's a solid strategy that people should consider for wealth building. These points are in no particular order.

1.   Leverage your time

The first reason why I think property development is a good strategy is because it is an awesome way to leverage your time. You can work less and get paid more. I believe you can run a small, multi-unit project by investing around 10-14 hours a week of your time and get back a few hundred thousand dollars in two years. That's a pretty good return on your time investment.

If you think about the time that you spend doing something and the financial reward that you get in return, I think you will find that property development can provide incredible leverage. What that means is, yes, you can do one project and spend, say, 14 hours a week. Or you could do multiple projects and do it full time to get exponential returns on your investment in your time. So, I think time leverage is a really good reason to consider getting into property development.

2.   Take charge of your financial destiny

The second reason is that property development is a great way for you to take charge of your financial destiny. Lots of things can happen in life. If you're working for somebody else, if you're an employee in an organisation, then you are always at risk of losing your job. That can be through no fault of your own. There can be corporate decisions made that lead to you no longer having a job. There can be huge upheavals in your industry that are beyond the control of the business that you work for.

We've all seen the impacts of the COVID-19 pandemic across the world. Certain industries and sectors were basically shut down overnight. If you worked in events or hospitality or the creative arts, a lot of work in those industries essentially disappeared instantly. It had nothing to do with the people in those industries. They were just victims of circumstance.

If you decide to get into property development, you can take charge of your financial destiny. It's up to you how much money you can make. You can do one project every couple of years and add some extra money to your superannuation fund or build up your property portfolio. In a relatively short period of time, you might find that you're actually financially secure.

So, I think taking charge of your financial destiny is a big reward for doing property development.

3.   Take your property investing to the next level

The third thing I like about property development is that it takes your property investing to the next level. I suspect that if you're reading this book, you probably already have an interest in property, you're probably already a property investor, and you're potentially looking to take your investing to the next level. You may have already bought a couple of investment properties. Maybe you started out with a small unit, and you bought a bigger property. Then you purchased a better property and so on.

That's the standard journey of a property investor, but you're reliant upon the performance of the market to do the heavy lifting for capital growth. Some people add value by doing renovations, but the vast majority of uplift tends to come from market movements.

As investors become more comfortable with property investing and the associated risks, they consider taking things to the next level through property development and proactively manufacturing better returns.

4.   Manufacture growth and equity

As I just covered, property development is a natural evolution of the property investment journey. A lot of people look to property development to take their investing to the next level because it enables them to manufacture growth in their investments. You can take a piece of land and turn it into multiple income producing assets, which you can use to create cash flow. Or you can sell down the new units and enjoy the profits. Alternatively, you could sell one and retain one with low gearing or maybe even debt free.

I don't think there's many quicker ways to achieve that in property without adding value through a significant renovation. I got into development because I like the idea of manufacturing growth. I don't want to wait for the market to do the heavy lifting, and funnily enough, I basically skipped the whole property investing part and just went straight into the developing bit. My first purchase of a property was actually a development site, but for most people they're probably already investing in property and can see development as a way to generate growth and equity in a smart and methodical way.

5.   Flexibility to build strong assets

The next point about why development can be a good strategy is because you have flexibility about the kind of assets that you build. You could build a portfolio of cash flow producing properties at wholesale prices, whether that be high yielding rooming houses, duplexes, or other types of property that are good at producing cash flow. Instead of trying to find them, you can just manufacture them.

It also means that you can provide a specific product to a specific market. If you're already investing, or own investment property in a particular suburb or area, you probably understand that market. You may see that there's a demand for a particular type of product that isn't being provided in that marketplace, so you could go ahead and manufacture it and deliver something that renters or buyers actually want.

6.   Strong demand for infill developments

The next point that I would make about why property development is a good strategy is because I think there's going to be strong ongoing demand in Australia for infill developments in metropolitan and regional areas as the population continues to grow.

Infill basically means developing an existing residential block into something with more dwellings on it than before. So, you can take a standard residential block with one house and put two or three or four units on it. Australia is still a fairly young country in terms of our population and density. Fortunately, we are a growing nation, which means we need to keep expanding our population to boost our economy and we've got the space to do it.

The Australian federal government wants to attract people to Australia to help pay taxes. We have an ageing population, which means a big cohort of baby boomers are going to move from being taxpayers to tax takers over the next few decades. They're going to stop paying taxes and they're going to start drawing from services offered by government. In order to pay for that, the government is going to have to keep bringing in younger, tax-paying people to grow the economy and sustain our tax base.

For all the arguments about whether Australia should or should not be a big population nation, the fact is that it has to keep growing its population to underpin the economy. Expect governments to keep bringing migrants into the country, along with locals who continue to invest and upgrade, and you will have a healthy number of people looking for a place to buy. I think there's going to be an ongoing demand for property developments in metropolitan (and regional) areas, particularly infill style developments, which are perfectly suited for the smaller developer.

Added on top of all that is the fact that Aussies love buying property. There is a culture around property ownership or residential property ownership in Australia, and I don't see that changing anytime soon. All of that working together is going to lead to ongoing demand for residential property in Australia.

7.   Boost your retirement fund

Property development could be good for boosting your retirement fund. For example, if you currently own a residential block of land somewhere in Australia, you might be able to develop your own land and realise the potential financial gains right underneath your feet. You could then use that money to boost your retirement fund in a highly tax efficient way.

You might be able to make a couple of hundred thousand dollars (or even more) and throw it into your superannuation and really bump up your retirement funds. It might make a huge difference to your quality of life as you head off into retirement.

8.   Create extra wealth

Property development can create extra wealth. You might just be able to do the odd project here and there every couple of years for a bit of extra income. Maybe you have a bit of extra time, or you've got a bit of extra money, and every couple of years you just bank the profits from a project. Over 10 years you might earn an extra $500,000, $700,000, or more.

That extra money compounds over time and could be worth well over a million dollars just from spending 10-14 hours a week working on a project. You don't even have to wait for retirement. You could just use it to support your lifestyle. Use those project profits every couple of years to take yourself off on a nice holiday or buy a new car, whatever it is that tickles your fancy.

9. Leave a legacy

Another point that's worth considering with property development is around creating a legacy. You can set up a trust and within that trust, you can have properties that provide income and financial returns long past your lifetime. You could support future generations of people.

Your grandchildren's children could benefit from your efforts. Maybe you set up a trust to provide assistance with education costs. That could be a pretty amazing legacy to leave behind for your family. The prospect of leaving a legacy is something that inspires some people to create wealth and make it available to future generations.

10. Property developing is repeatable

A point I like about property development is that it's repeatable. Once you understand the property development process and the project life cycle, you can just do it all again. The process doesn't change. It's just the bumps along the way that are always a little bit different. It's something that's not only repeatable, but also a lifelong skill.

Once you know how to develop property and go through the property development process, it's like riding a bike. You never really forget how to do it. You just have to follow the steps and get the right people to help you.

Over 20, 30, 40 years, imagine how many projects you could do, even on a casual basis. You could do 14 or 15 little projects without too much drama. Imagine how much additional wealth that could bring you as it compounds in a superannuation fund or in another investment vehicle.

Also, if you kept recycling your capital and slowly putting it into projects and building up your cash, your wealth could grow to be pretty significant.

11. Property development is fulfilling

Property development can be very satisfying and fulfilling. There is something special about having an idea, having a vision for a site, and then slowly bringing it to realisation. It feels fulfilling to work through all the challenges along the way and then deliver new properties to the market. Building something tangible that's most likely going to be there for decades is actually very rewarding. It's something that you can walk past and point to and say, I did that. I think there is a special, glorious feeling that a lot of people get when they finish a property development. It is partly why people become quite enamoured with it and look to get more heavily into property developing once they get started.

Off the back of that, it's actually scalable. We talked about how you could do multiple projects, and it's not as hard as people think it might be. Certainly, no harder than working nine to five in a job that perhaps doesn't inspire you.

12. Build a big business with low overheads

The next thing I like about property development as a strategy is that you can build a big business with almost no staff and very low overheads. You can outsource most of the skills required to consultants and other people. You don't need to have a fancy office. You don't need to have lots of staff.

You can actually keep your operating costs to a fairly low level. As I just mentioned, it can be scalable. You can focus on one style of development like a three- or four-unit project and keep doing it to become a master of that type of development. Then ultimately, you can have a profitable business once you work on getting that cash flow happening. It can be a model that can underpin a good business with reasonably low overhead costs.

13. Not that risky

The final point that I would make about why property development can be a good wealth strategy is that I think it can be reasonably low risk. Once you know what you're doing, you can actually mitigate quite a bit of the risk involved with developing. You may not eliminate all the risk, but you could certainly get it down to a level that you would feel comfortable with. We will talk more about risk in chapter seven.

Considering the financial rewards that can come with a good project, the risk-to-reward ratio can be very appealing.

Those are some of the key reasons that I think property development can be a really good investment strategy that people can use to grow their wealth and maybe become a million-dollar property developer.

5. Common types of property development in Australia

*"I had no ambition to make a fortune. Mere money making
has never been my goal, I had an ambition to build."*
John D. Rockefeller

What is property development? In its simplest form, I think it is about adding value to a property, so it is worth more than before. That could be a simple renovation or building a high-rise tower. It may be taking a tract of farmland and creating smaller parcels of land through a subdivision. There are numerous ways to develop property, but for the purposes of this book we are going to focus and talk about the smaller, simpler, more common projects. The ones accessible to the fledgling developer. I am not covering renovations as a strategy in this book, we are talking pure development projects.

Here are some examples of projects at the lower end of the developing spectrum:

Backyard subdivision - slice out some land from an existing parcel of land and sell off as a new lot (potentially build a dwelling on it and then sell as a house and land package). I think this area will enjoy more relaxed planning rules over time as governments look to make it easier for landowners to unlock land and create new housing options on suburban lots in areas with existing services.

For example, New South Wales has streamlined processes for building 'granny flats' in backyards.

Duplex projects - take one parcel of land, divide the land in two, and build two units on each new parcel. These often share a common wall down the middle to make efficient use of the land. You can sell them separately. Or maybe 'split' the block and sell the land lots separately.

Small unit projects - take a larger residential block of land and slice it up into smaller lots and build multiple units/townhouses on each new parcel of land. The project gets built all at the same time and residents share a common driveway. The units often share walls on the edges of lots. Popular smaller projects are three- and four-unit developments referred to as infill developments, as they are projects done within existing residential areas.

Specialised residential projects - using the above methods to build high cash flow producing dwellings such as rooming houses, disability accommodation, or retirement living.

Small boutique apartment projects - like a low rise building with less than 15-20 apartments. These are becoming increasingly common in inner metropolitan areas as they are a very efficient way to use land. They will continue to grow in popularity as population growth and urbanisation continues in bigger cities. People want to live close to lifestyle amenities like shops, restaurants, and transport links.

There are many twists and variations on the above, which is part of the excitement and dynamism of property development. There are lots of ways to create value. Some are straightforward, while others are complex. Usually, the less complex and risky the project, the less profit you make, like anything in life.

So, there are plenty of choices depending on your risk appetite, money raising skills, and creativity. I suggest starting small and growing from there.

6. Property Developer Training

"Those who don't know must learn from those who do."
Plato

I had the ambition to help people get into property development since before my first project finished. Which, back then, was probably naked enthusiasm from the enjoyment I had experienced getting my first project underway. It was such a satisfying journey.

There is a real sense of accomplishment when you take an idea from imagination to reality. I've felt this on every property development project thus far. A completed project is something that has a glory and legacy to it. The property you build, will in all likelihood, be around for decades. Lots of different people will probably live there. Memories will be created there. Futures imagined. Lives lived.

Sharing knowledge

However, I felt I needed more experience before I could start helping other people. So, I got going on some other projects, and I started my podcast, the Property Developer Podcast. Check it out at www.propertydeveloperpodcast. com for great conversations with property developers and other people in the property industry.

When I started the podcast, it was a thing of pure love. It still is. Before launching the podcast, and when I was getting started in developing, I was going around talking to people about development because I was hungry to learn from people who were in the game.

I kept having these amazing conversations with great people and they shared so much gold. Each conversation had little nuggets of information that still stick with me today. Yet it was only me that was taking away the lessons, and that was one reason why I started the podcast.

I wanted to share what I learned with other people because developing can be a bit of a closed shop. People in the industry have won expensive and painful skills and experience, which they want to protect. Which I totally get. I too have won some expensive and painful skills and experience.

In any case, I wanted to share the conversations I was having with interesting people because when I was getting started, I was hungry for information about developing, but it was hard to find.

You would get the occasional episode on a property investing or real estate podcast but there was no dedicated show about property developing. In fact, that's how I got the bright idea of doing property development.

I heard a guy on a podcast talking about developing and that's when the lightbulb went off. That's when I realised property developing was what I wanted to get into. Once I left my 'safe' job, one of the first things I did was launch my podcast.

Starting transmission

In 2016, I started the world's first regular podcast about property development and many years later it is still going strong. It has been such an amazing way for me to connect with some interesting people, learn incredible lessons and most importantly, talk about developing.

Without the podcast, it is highly unlikely I would have been able to speak with heads of major development companies, former FBI hostage negotiators, and terrific people doing great projects. Some big, many small. Each guest on my show brings a little nugget, or in some cases, seams of gold, in the form of insight, tips, and ideas.

One of the other reasons I started the podcast was because I had come to realise that developing can be somewhat of a lonely game. As I often like to say, being a developer is like being a conductor of the orchestra. You are up front directing the ensemble and keeping everyone in time so that a wonderful tune can be produced by the group. But, you are not down in the orchestra pit with the musicians.

Being a property developer means being the captain of the ship. You call the shots, keep everyone working together, and make sure that stuff gets done when it is needed and to a good standard. In fact, a project requires a big team that you must coordinate. There's only one person who has the aerial view of what is going on and that's you.

Lonely at the top

Only you know all the issues that are currently happening. Only you know fully where the most risk is. Only you know of all the challenges and hurdles you overcame to get the project finished. It is impossible to share all those trials and tribulations with anybody else because they are unique to you and the project.

But other developers will understand. They will appreciate the things you are going through or that you have been through to make it to the other side. I imagine professional sportspeople feel that way, or Olympians. Only others who have been through the same thing can really appreciate the pain and sacrifice they have made along the way.

The hard training sessions, the fatigue, the moments of doubt, the setbacks, and the injuries, they all amplify the joy of success because all the challenges make the success feel so good. If it was easy, it would not be special or rewarding. If everybody could be a developer and make millions of dollars, then guess what? They would.

It's the barriers to entry that actually help you. If you can push through the challenges and obstacles then you can get to the other side and enjoy that feeling of accomplishment, the financial rewards and sense of achievement.

I often remind myself of the barriers when I face a challenge. If I am facing this issue and it is a common one, like delays with councils, then other people must be having the same trouble. Some of those people are going to drop out of the race, give up after one project, or even fold mid-project. It will all be too much for them because they were not prepared. They didn't know what they were going to come up against. They were expecting easy peasy, and instead they got life.

One outcome from the podcast was the regular emails I started to receive from listeners who were grateful for the content about developing. The fact that someone was "pulling back the kimono" as Steve Jobs once said. It was inspiring people to get started in property development or for active developers to take their development business to the next level.

Enough experience

A nagging issue I kept experiencing whenever I thought about helping people was a sense that I wouldn't be able to help people enough. Another concern I had was around the type of people that might want to get involved with developing. Frankly, many people have a fantasy about property development and becoming a property developer. They think it is the golden path to easy riches.

These people think you just buy a block of land, get a permit, build the properties, sell them, and boom, you bank a million dollars. The toughest choice after that is deciding which colour Lamborghini to buy or which luxury foreign holiday destination to head to.

I didn't want to deal with unrealistic fantasists. I didn't want to promote a false hope and talk about making millions with online ads featuring Ferraris and private jets. I wanted content that didn't require me to fudge returns to sound cool.

My lived experience, and the experience of most developers I know, is nothing like those kinds of fantasies that get peddled by some people. Sure, you can make millions through property development. You can make millions in one project. My first project did in fact achieve that, but that's not where most people start (okay, except for me but that was unexpected, unplanned, and unusual).

Most small-scale property developments like a duplex or a three- or four-unit project can make a couple of hundred thousand dollars. This is still a lot of money, and for the time you need to invest it is an amazing return. You would be amazed at how little time a project can take to manage, if you know what you are doing.

Fast money

The fantasy developers are the people who run the back of the napkin feaso. Buy price $1 million. Build price $2 million. Sell price $4 million. Boom. $1 million in profit. They have no idea what they are doing, and they look for the quick and easy buck.

Now, property development can be lucrative. It can make great returns, but it is a get rich quicker scheme, not a get rich quick scheme. You can create a pile of cash or build a substantial property portfolio over time (at wholesale cost) much faster than the traditional buy and hold strategy. There's nothing wrong with the traditional buy and hold strategy. It just takes time.

Personally, that traditional path takes too long, and requires the market to do the heavy lifting over a cycle or two. Property development can accelerate this process by manufacturing growth and get you to the same wealth point faster than buying and holding. It is not for everybody and there's nothing wrong with the buy and hold strategy, it just depends on how you like to do things.

It is quite common for people to start out on their property investment journey by starting small and buying a unit. They build some equity, and then they reinvest to buy another property. After a while they become comfortable with what they are doing and then they start to think about taking it up a notch, accelerating the capital growth, and manufacturing returns. That's when they look to property development to take that next step. It's a common property investment ascension pathway.

Attracting the right people

I was wary of attracting the wrong crowd. Then one day I had a realisation. I didn't need to promote property development in the way that many people or spruikers like to. The fast cars and fancy lifestyle. The get rich quick mentality it fosters, and the false hope it gives people. The sense of deflation some people must feel when they realise what's involved. It's not all strawberries and cream. You actually need to work for your results.

Fledgling developers could avoid paying a small fortune chasing an illusion with some better information and affordable education.

I didn't need to falsify what's possible or inflate what can be achieved in say five years. I could just tell it plainly and simply, outline what's involved and what's possible, in my own style.

If people like what they read from this book or hear on my podcast and become serious about getting into development, they can do an affordable online course which gives them a very solid foundation to work from. The training provides everything people need to get started on their first project.

Training for fledgling developers

I put together the Property Developer Training program because I know that property development can transform your life and I can show you how to do it. I'm doing it myself. I believe the course is exceptional value for the money and can help people decide if developing is really something they want to tackle, without investing massive dollars and attending boring weekend workshops.

You can jump straight into the training and do the modules in your own time and at your own pace, hang out with me and others who also want to get into property development, and who knows, maybe you will become the next million-dollar developer?

Imagine being able to add a couple of hundred thousand dollars to your income every two or three years, with less risk than you might think. What kind of difference could that make to your life? Pretty significant, I would think.

Depending on what's important to you, it could enable you to buy nice holidays, send your kids to private school, upgrade to a bigger home in a better suburb, buy a new car, boost your superannuation for retirement, help your elderly parents live more comfortably, buy a boat, go to space, build an orphanage, it's up to you. The possibilities are only defined by you.

Maybe you don't want to pocket the cash, maybe you want to amass a property portfolio at cost, 15-20 percent less than what you would pay in the open market. You could build up equity and then recycle that into another development project to add more property into your holdings.

You see, I believe that once you learn how to develop property in a systematic way, carefully finding and assessing opportunities, you will see that it is not as hard as you think. It is also not as easy as some people make out, but not beyond the capability and reach of many people.

You don't need Warren Buffet to fund you. You don't need a degree in construction. You don't need a master's in finance. You don't need to build the next Trump Tower. You don't need years of property investing experience (my first property purchase was a development site). You just need purpose, intention, and a healthy dose of resilience.

Once you complete your first project, the mystery of the process will disappear. The fog of uncertainty will lift, and it is highly likely that you will be raring to go again.

Champing at the bit

Most people I know who have completed their first development are champing at the bit to get started on their next project. Usually, they start thinking about how they can run multiple projects. It happened to me. I started on my second project before I finished my first because I knew I could do it.

That's the other beautiful thing about property development. It is a repeatable process and a lifelong skill. You can keep developing property well into your senior years and I'm sure for some people it becomes a hobby as they move into their 'retirement' era.

There are plenty of people who knock over a development every couple of years, pocket some profits, top up their lifestyle fund, and do it all again. Many first-time developers get bitten by the development bug and start looking to take it a few steps further and try to make it a full-time gig. Whatever is your jam it's up to you. I believe that having options in life is a luxury worth pursuing.

Imagine what earning an extra million dollars or more over the next five to ten years would be like for your life? It's really not that hard to do through low risk, small scale property developments. What would your superannuation fund look like in 10, 20, 30 years with all that extra cash compounding away? How might your property portfolio look? How might your life transform? It's pretty exciting and totally achievable.

Be sure to head over to www.propertydevelopertraining.com and check out what's covered in the course. If you decide to get started, then be sure to use the promo code 'book' to get a big fat discount. Do it now, and I will see you in there.

7. Fear and risk

"I am an old man and have had many
worries, but most have never come to pass."
Marcus Aurelius

One of, if not the biggest, obstacles to people trying new things in life is the fear of change. Fear drives a lot of human decision making. Fear of failing. Fear of loss. Fear of rejection. Fear of success. Often it just boils down to the fear of the unknown. We tend to project the worst-case scenario, and that's what stops people from quitting their jobs (if they hate it), trying something new, and going after their dreams.

Fear is what stops lots of people from getting into property development. Fear of losing money is probably fear number one. This is a well-placed fear. It is very easy to blow money on a development project. You buy the wrong property expecting to be able to build three units on it only to find out it has a single dwelling covenant on it. Or you buy in the wrong zone that doesn't support the type of project you want to do. There are plenty of ways to lose money in property development, but that's the same in any business, especially if you don't know what you are doing.

Therein lies the key. Knowing what you are doing. If you know the pitfalls to look out for, if you have a plan for what you are going to do, then it is less scary. Once you have completed a project, the fog of mystery lifts and you realise that many of your fears didn't materialise. I don't mind a bit of fear driving you, as it keeps you on your toes. I'm still conscious of the risks in developing and like to stay alert to the dangers. Fear doesn't drive me, but I am aware of the risks. It keeps me focused on what to get right.

Fear of losing money

I would say much of the fear of losing money and failing leads us back to education. If you can learn the key elements of property development, then you can focus on getting them right. It's like learning to drive. You wouldn't expect a learner to jump into a race car and know how to handle it. You start out in a small to medium-sized car, getting a feel for the wheel to understand what you need to look out for, staying alert to other motorists and pedestrians. As you become more comfortable with driving, you start to operate subconsciously, but you are still alert to all the important aspects of driving. After that, moving into different types of vehicles is less daunting, as you know how to maneuver a vehicle and handle the roads.

It is one of the reasons why I created the Property Developer Training, so you could be aware of what you need to know about property development, how you can get yourself set up for success, and how to avoid the common pitfalls that trap people. The checklists and guides help you stay on track and minimise the risk of making an avoidable mistake. Head over to www.propertydevelopertraining.com and check out everything that is included in the training. Use the promo code 'book' to get a big fat discount.

Fling off fear

What I suggest people do if they are afraid of changing or making a decision is to write down all the outcomes they fear might happen. Next to them, write down all the things that can be done to mitigate that from happening. This is exactly what I did as my first project got bigger and bigger. I wrote down the key fears I had - losing money, going broke, not being able to sell the properties at a high enough price, etc. I worked out what I could do to address these fears.

Here's an example of how you can map out your fears/concerns and see what you can do to mitigate the fear/concern.

Fear/Concerns	Mitigation
Finished product doesn't sell for prices predicted or sells for well below budget	- Thorough research of local market to ensure realistic sales prices and market demand for product - Speak with every selling agent in the local area to determine realistic sales price - Run 5% and 10% sensitivity analysis in feasibility to determine profit if product sells for less - Aim for $70-80k in profit per unit so you have lots of room to drop before making a loss - Engage multiple local agents for sales campaign via conjunction sales agreement - Engage project marketer to sell stock if struggling with local agents

When you really think it through, there is a lot that can be put in place to stop the worst outcome from occurring. Plenty of studies have shown that usually the worst-case scenario rarely comes to pass, even though we worry about it most. Think about your own life. Can you recall a period of being really worried about something bad happening and in the end it all worked out and wasn't such a big deal after all? On my first project none of my worst fears came to pass. Hooray!

I also think that people have a fear of succeeding. What if you become a really successful property developer? What then? You will have a different set of obligations and responsibilities. A new range of issues to deal with. Is that what you really want? Are you ready for them?

Don't let fear drive your decision making or stop you from taking a new turn if that's what you really want. Focus on what would inspire you and go for that.

Which brings us to risk.

Risky business?

Okay, let's talk about risk because I don't think risk is something that people think about enough or otherwise, they think about it too much. In a nutshell, property development is all about managing risk and looking at ways to minimise, mitigate, or eliminate risk. Be that through thorough research, engaging top notch consultants, and/or learning from others.

Funnily enough, property development is really a people game. There are people involved at every stage of the project. The people around you can help to reduce the risks. Relationships make a huge difference in continuing to deliver successful projects. When you find good people, stick with them, and they will help you avoid, and maybe get you out of, some holes.

So, what are the risks involved in doing property development? Remember, there are risks involved in doing anything, including doing nothing. There are risks involved in simply investing in property. Say you buy an existing property and rent it out, there's risk involved with that. You buy something in an area that doesn't grow in value the way that you thought it would. You get tenants who trash the place. There are risks with any kind of investment, but we can often identify them and take steps to mitigate them.

A lot of the risks in developing can be identified at the start and they correspond with each phase of the development cycle. Let's have a look at these key risks:

- Profit risk - will the project be profitable?

- Planning risk - can you achieve the planning outcome you expect?

- Market risk - will the market soften or go backwards before you finish?

- Sales risk - will you be able to sell your product at the price you project?

- Construction risk - will you be able to build your new dwelling at the price you expect and without cost blowouts or the builder going bust?

- Settlement risk - will the buyers settle on their sales?

- Finance risk - will you be able to obtain finances to buy the land and then construct the new dwellings?

Profit risk

Many of the risks above can be identified and mitigated through solid project preparation, analysis, and site due diligence. If we look at the steps in the development process, we can identify what the most likely risks are.

For example, at the very beginning of a project when you are looking at buying a site, we want to ensure it ends up being profitable. We can mitigate the risk of that not happening by doing a really good due diligence on the site.

I cover the importance of due diligence in my training, including doing a great feasibility, understanding the sales prices in the area, the purchase price of the land, the likely resale price of the new properties, the construction costs, and all the other costs for the project. If we can identify and price most of those, we can know what the likely outcome is. If we do the right research and preparation, then we can have confidence in our projections. Hit and hope is not the preferred strategy in property development!

Planning risk

Let's look at planning risk. What's the likelihood of us getting a planning permit for what we're proposing to do? Again, this comes back to working with your team and your town planner around the likelihood of success.

If you're looking to do something pretty standard in an area where there's lots of people already doing that, there should be a clear and recent precedent. So, the risk of you not getting a permit is pretty low and it's probably not something to worry about.

However, if you plan on doing a four-unit development in a quiet street where the zoning doesn't support more intense development, then you might be in for a rude shock.

This is part of your due diligence process which ensures you buy in the right location.

Market risk

If we have a look at market risk, this gets a bit tricky because we have no control over the market. What happens if the market drops five percent or 10 percent? Can you sustain that kind of fall? Perhaps you can hold off on starting the project if the market is softening before you commence construction. Instead of selling all the completed properties, you might rent them out and wait for the market to improve.

Maybe you are prepared to take a lower profit to ensure you don't lose any money. If you can think about it ahead of time, you can be strategically prepared when it happens, and it won't be the shock it might have been.

You can include a sensitivity analysis in your feasibility to show the impact of a five percent drop, or a five percent gain, and use that to determine what level of movement you are comfortable with.

Sales risk

Which brings us to sales risk. Like before, you must talk to agents in the area, look at the depth of the market that you're moving into, and look at recent sales data. How likely is it that you'll be able to sell something at the price that you need to sell?

If you're talking about selling something at the mid-range of the market, then what are the market rates for that sort of property? If you are in the mid-range, then you'd probably say the risk is pretty low. If your feasibility says that you need to sell a standard new townhouse or property for five percent or 10 percent more than everything else that's similar, even though it's no bigger or with no better inclusions, then that's unlikely to happen.

You are setting yourself up for failure there, but you might think, "well, we're actually going to do something bigger with better finishes, the bathroom is going to be bigger, the kitchen is going to have superior materials. Our inclusions are going to be better." However, it will likely cost you more to build that product so your construction cost will probably be higher too, which you need to factor in.

From talking with salespeople, they might agree that you could achieve five percent above the median sales price with better inclusions and a larger living area.

Again, it's about having that intelligence and doing the research to find out what's realistic to determine how risky it is and the likelihood of it being successful.

Construction risk

The next one is construction risk. What's the risk of your builder going bust or things blowing out the budget? I talk about this in the Property Developer Training, about how you can find a really good builder and how you can take steps to ensure that they aren't going to go bust, that they are the right person for the job.

Now, sometimes things just happen and they are beyond your control. Like a builder going bust or costs rising unexpectedly. But there's steps you can take to mitigate the likelihood of that happening, like investigating the builder, looking at their other projects and talking to their past and present clients.

You can investigate if they've had any issues with the building authorities or other regulators. How long have they been around, how long have their key staff worked there, who owns the company? Those kinds of things can help to discover what shape the builder is in.

You can compare what their prices are like with other builders. If their price seems pretty reasonable for what you're asking for, not over the top but not way under then that's a good sign.

During 2021 and into 2022, building costs were escalating at an incredible rate and causing issues with builders and developers managing their construction costs. In a situation like this it would be prudent to add some additional buffer to your construction contingency allowance and bump it up by an extra three to five percent.

This is a wise way to offset the risk of unexpected cost blowouts.

If the builder has been around for 10, 15, 20 years, then they will be able to discuss relevant industry issues like escalating construction costs and how to mitigate them. Again, we've done something to mitigate the construction risk by taking steps to ensure that we've picked the right builder.

Settlement risk

At the end of the project, you start talking about settlement risk (although really this is set up from your sales efforts). What's the likelihood of people not actually settling? I haven't had any issues with settlements falling over. Part of the reason for that is that our buyers are predominantly owner occupiers, and they are really keen to move into their new homes. They were serious about buying and don't want to lose their hard saved deposits.

If you are selling to home occupiers in a certain market, and by talking with local selling agents, you might establish that the settlement risk is quite low. The agents say they don't really see many people defaulting on their purchases and it's probably not likely to happen. It is not impossible but unlikely.

It might be a different story if you're building a big apartment tower and many of your buyers are investors or foreigners. If the market drops five or 10 percent, they might just walk away and you have limited recourse.

This has happened in recent memory; it happened a lot in 2019. Market shifts are beyond our control. That's why banks ask for a 10 percent deposit because they know from experience that if someone does walk away, you can use that 10 percent deposit to then run a sales campaign to sell your unit. You've got a 10 percent buffer to play with.

The idea is that you're less likely to lose out compared to the previous sale.

Having a 10 percent deposit helps mitigate the settlement risk.

Sales agents have an important role to play in bringing in qualified and reliable buyers who will settle their transaction when the time comes.

Finance risk

The other risk to consider is finance risk. Are you confident that you will have the cash to complete the project? Will you be able to obtain funding to purchase the site? Will you be able to obtain construction funding to build the new properties?

Again, you can consider ways to mitigate this risk. You can speak with finance brokers before you start the project about the lending market. You should learn what sorts of terms and conditions are common, so you know what you need to satisfy before applying for those loans.

You can work out the cash you need to finish the project by doing a great financial analysis to determine the amount of money you need to raise before you get started. Figuring out how much cash you need at each stage of the project and working out if you can secure that cash when you need it is vital.

So, you can sit down and identify all those key risk points and work out the things that you can do to mitigate them. But again, don't forget, there's risk in everything, there's risk in not doing something. You just need to understand what's your risk profile. What are you prepared to risk?

I have a reasonable risk tolerance but that doesn't mean that I'm just prepared to do anything. I'm not willing to just easily lose money. In fact I hate losing money. But I'm prepared to try and push things a little bit, maybe in the planning phase or the marketing phase, to see if we can get a little bit more for our sales prices. I understand that and I'm prepared to take that risk.

Sometimes that doesn't work out as planned, as I have discovered, but sometimes it's successful too. So, understand your risk profile and understand what you need to do or what you can do to mitigate those risks.

I have found that property developing is not as risky as people might think, providing you do the work around knowing how a project will unfold. Usually, the perception of developing being risky comes from people who don't have any experience doing a property development project.

I will repeat again that developing is not without risk. But if you go into a project with your eyes open and with a strategic approach, using foresight instead of hindsight, it might just be less risky than you expect.

Take a look at my Property Developer Training program if you would like to understand the lifecycle of a project, what you need to do along the way, and how to run a great feasibility. Go to www.propertydevelopertraining.com and use the code 'book' for a discount.

8. Cash flow

"A cultivated mind is one to which the fountains of knowledge have been opened, and which has been taught, in any tolerable degree, to exercise its faculties."
John Stuart Mill

One of the challenges with doing property development, unlike other businesses, is the issue of cash flow. All businesses rely on cash flow but with a property development project you basically don't have any cash flow during a project. It's pretty much all outflow.

When you're doing a project, you're spending on all your costs and waiting until the project's finished to get your returns. Property development is a cash-intensive business.

My projects face those classic cash flow challenges. In an interview we did for my podcast, one of the guests Rod Fehring, the former CEO of Frasers Property Australia (which is a very big property development company), said to me, "that if you don't have cash flow, then you don't have a business". That has really stuck with me. While I do generate fees and cash flow from managing projects, I'd like to see more flows of cash through my business. Who wouldn't, right?

Part of the reason I offer a training program is to help with my cash flow. I think it's a win-win situation though, because people get access to an affordable program showing them how to do property development. Participants can then go and start their first project, aware of the key issues and pitfalls to avoid, earn money, and enjoy themselves.

In return for sharing my knowledge, I get paid for showing people how to do a successful development. That's a win for me, and a win for them. It helps with my cash flow, and it helps them potentially realise an amazing life.

Cash flow was one reason for me to produce the training program, but a funny thing happened after I launched the Property Developer Training. I started getting emails from people who had been through the program saying how much they enjoyed it and how much they learned. They could see how property development could really change their lives. One guy was going through the modules with his 15-year-old son, and planned on doing a project together. How awesome is that!

After I got a few of these emails, I have to admit that I got the warm tingles down my neck, and I realised that I could potentially help thousands of people take control of their financial destiny through property development. The number of people I can help through the training is exponentially more than the number of projects I can manage. So why not dedicate some of my time to helping people transform their lives through property development, just like me? It seems like a win all around. So that's what I have been doing.

I still make fees from managing projects, I enjoy capital events when profits are realised, and I earn money from helping people learn about development. Like any entrepreneur and businessperson, I am interested in ways of generating extra cash flow and income, and you should be too. Once you are up and running with doing projects you will start to see the opportunities to generate money and income and get your cash flow pumping.

In chapter 11 on how to become a full-time developer, I outline some of the ways you can generate cash flow as a property developer.

9. The financial feasibility

"Analyse data just so far as to obtain simplicity and no further."
Henri Poincare

If you want to become a million-dollar property developer, then you need to get across the financial analysis of a project. How will you know what the expected profit is without accounting for all the costs and revenue? So, let's take a look at the financial analysis of a property development project, and go through how you start to put together a financial feasibility (feaso) for your project.

We're going to cover financial analysis basics, the big three numbers that are important for your feasibility, and details of project costs. In the Property Developer Training, I've put together a feasibility template for you that makes it easy to work through all these points.

There are many ways of doing a feasibility and various templates for laying out an analysis. You can find plenty of them online. So, don't be afraid to seek them out and have a look at them to see how different people lay them out. The important thing to remember is that a feaso is about capturing all the project costs and getting those numbers as accurate as you can.

The challenge that many people face when they're first doing a feasibility study is that one, they don't know what numbers to put in there, and two, they don't know how to get those numbers. In my training program, we address how you can start to pick up some of the numbers for consultants and other fees and go deeper into how you can track down the numbers that you need for your feasibility. Or, at least, allow you to determine a pretty good estimate.

In its essence, a feasibility is a financial snapshot of how your project is going to perform and it is just a statement of your expenses less your income, which will give you (hopefully) a profit. When a broker or a finance person presents your project to a lender, this is basically how they're going to present it to them, along with a supportive narrative about your strengths as a borrower. It outlines your projected income, the expenses, and where all the money is going to go.

A feaso is only as good as the inputs (ie the numbers) that go into it, so it's important that you work as hard as you can to get the numbers as accurate as possible.

The following is a feasibility for an imaginary four-unit project to highlight the key elements of a feasibility. Behind these top line numbers is a lot of work and a bunch of other figures that feed up to the Profit and Loss statement.

PROFIT & LOSS

INCOME/REVENUE

Rent	**$10,000**	
Gross realisation value (total Sales)	**$2,095,000**	
less cost of commission	**$41,900**	
less GST on sale* (using margin scheme)	**$137,773**	
Total revenue		**$1,925,327**

EXPENSES

Acquisition Costs	**$579,500**	
Design and Planning Costs	**$41,040**	
Construction Costs (incl 5% contingency)	**$750,348**	
Contributions and Charges	**$57,000**	
Holding Costs	**$8,685**	
Legal Fees	**$7,380**	
Finance Costs	**$84,339**	
Other finance costs	**$4,995**	
Sales and Marketing Costs	**$7,335**	
Total expenses		**$1,540,622**

Bonds refunded	**$5,000**	
		$5,000

NET PROFIT (Net Income)		**$389,705**
Margin		**25.30%**

Total Development Cost (ex GST)	**$1,540,622**	
Gross realisation value (total sales)	**$2,095,000**	

Let's just take a closer look at the feasibility. Up in the top section, the **INCOME/REVENUE** line, we've got our income and revenue, funnily enough. We put in here any rent that we might collect on the property while we're getting our planning permit or before it gets demolished.

The **gross realisation value** (GRV) is the total sales of your finished new properties when they are finished and settled. Thus, the four new units we've said are going to be built will be worth just over $2 million. Then we take away the costs of generating that revenue. Which is the cost of **commissions.** That's the sales agents commission of around $41,000 (based on a certain percentage of the value of the sale, say two percent) and then **GST** (Goods and Services Tax) of $137,773 on the sale using the margin scheme. We will talk briefly about the margin scheme in the coming pages.

Accounting for it all

One of the key people on your team is going to be an accountant, and this is another moment when you want to talk to them about the intent of your project. Are you planning on keeping any of your stock or are you selling everything for profit? Because that's going to influence some numbers, particularly the GST figure, and whether you claim GST along the way or how your profit is going to be treated. You should have that early conversation with your accountant about what you intend on doing, because it will influence the numbers in your feasibility. In this case, we are going to sell all of the stock for profit.

Our total revenue figure is $1,925,327. From that, we deduct all the expenses related to the project, and there are many. We have our **Acquisition Costs, Design and Planning Costs, Construction Costs, Contributions and Charges, Holding Costs, Legal Fees,**

Finance Costs, Other Finance Costs and Sales and Marketing Costs.

As you can see, there are lots of costs with doing a property development project, and it tallies up to $1,540,622 of total expenses.

Under expenses you will see a line just around refunding any bonds that you might have to initially lay out for asset protection or other reasons but that you should get back at the end of the project.

Profitable endeavour

To get our profit we subtract the costs and the expenses from our total revenue. In this example, that gives us a profit of $389,705. Another popular way of expressing the profitability of a project is to look at the return as a percentage of costs, which gives us our profit margin.

We get the margin by dividing the net profit by the total development costs or the total expenses, which gives us 25.3 percent. A pretty good return on our investment over two years and an excellent return for the cash we actually put into the deal. This is where the leverage of property development can really start to show dividends, because to get that $389,705 profit, we may have only had to put in $500,000 or $600,000. So, our cash-on-cash return for a $500,000 investment would be 77 percent or 64 percent for our $600,000 cash investment. Now you are talking solid returns!

At the bottom of the feasibility, you will see the total development costs (TDC) figure. That's the total costs of doing the project. That's everything that we've had to spend money on. Then the gross realisation value (GRV) which, as we've mentioned above, is the total sales. I'm going to cover more about why those two numbers are important in a little bit.

You will see that the big three numbers in your feasibility are the GRV, the acquisition costs (the cost of buying the land), and the construction costs. They are the big three numbers in your feasibility. You can see why it's important to get those ones right.

There are obviously a whole bunch of other costs that do add up and can make a difference to your bottom line but the big three, let's call them the holy trinity, have the biggest impact. You need to work really hard to try and get those numbers as accurate as you can. I go through the financials of a project in more depth in the Property Developer Training, this is a bit of skim across it.

Capturing the costs

Here's a quick summary of what all the expenses are for.

The **acquisition costs** are the costs involved with buying the land. The **design and planning costs** are all the things that you need to do to get your planning permit. The **construction costs** are obviously for getting the project built. **Contributions and charges** are for all the various authorities like water authorities, power authorities, and councils that make you pay a contribution to them for the privilege of using their network. They can really add up.

If you've invested in property, you'll be familiar with **Holding costs,** the various costs required to hold a property like insurance etc. **Legal fees** are for the various legal costs that you will incur, like getting contracts reviewed and prepared. **Finance costs** are where we pick up the interest for our initial land purchase and then also any interest for the construction loan. **Other finance costs** will be the things that you have to pay along the way to keep your business running, like accounting fees and other business costs. Finally, **sales and marketing** are the costs that you'll incur for promoting and marketing your new project.

That's your feasibility or profit and loss in a nutshell. I'll just say it again. In its simplest form, a feasibility is just a statement of the revenue less the expenses, which will hopefully give you a profit.

We've just looked at the basics of a financial statement. We've talked about the holy trinity of the big three numbers, which is the gross realisation value (GRV), the total cost of new sales, the acquisition costs from buying the land and the construction costs. We've also looked at the other project costs since there are many of them that go into a project. I provide a list of them in the Property Developer Training feasibility template and explain how we need to account for them in our feasibility. Capturing all the costs for the project is vital to producing a clear picture of how the development should perform.

Other important considerations

Let's turn our attention to the concept of highest and best use, GST and tax considerations. Also, we will go over an explanation of the margin scheme and touch on contributions and fees.

Now, before we get into this, I'm going to remind you again that I am not an accountant, and I am not a financial advisor. I am also not a lawyer. I'm just sharing this information with you as something to consider, and it's important that you discuss these further with the people on your team who are qualified to talk to you about them. However, let's cover some of these topics so that you're aware of them.

Highest and best use

The term highest and best use is very common across the property development sector, and it basically means the most effective way to develop the land. The highest and best use doesn't just mean the number of units that you put on there. It's also the configuration of those units. How big are they going to be? How many bedrooms are they going to have? What kind of finish are they going to have? These are all the considerations you need to think about when you're working out what is the highest and best use of the block.

GST and Tax

GST and tax are other important considerations that you need to discuss with your accountant because what you decide to do at the beginning of a project will have implications on how GST and tax gets treated. If you're setting up an entity that's going to be GST registered, then you will be able to claim the GST that you pay along the way through refunds, which can be quite helpful for your project cash flow. But don't forget that you may also have to pay company tax on the profits at the end. That may result in some personal tax issues if you've got money flowing back to you, or back to a trust or entities that you're involved with. Again, early conversations with your accountant can resolve these questions.

It is vital that GST is accounted for in your feasibility. This will become important as you begin to seek construction funding. More on that shortly.

Following on from tax and GST, let's briefly cover the margin scheme. Now you should talk to your accountant about getting a better explanation than you do from me on what the margin scheme is, but basically, it's a way of reducing the amount of tax that you might have to pay on your project.

Let me give you a pretty simple explanation but please go online and find supplemental information through a video or other run down of it. The margin scheme is a way of bringing your tax liability down. For example, if you buy a block of land for $500,000 and you don't pay any GST on it because you bought it from someone like a mum and dad who are selling their old residential property. Then you have your gross realisation value for the project. Everything that you sell comes to about two million dollars. You can deduct the land cost from the GRV. So, you can take away the $500k off the two million and only pay tax on the $1.5 million.

Instead of paying roughly about $181,000 of tax on the two million, you'd only be paying $136,000 on the $1.5 million, which is money in your pocket rather than the taxman, which is always a better place for it to be!

Using the margin scheme can help you pay less tax and make more profit. Just make sure that you talk to your accountant about whether or not it applies and how it affects you.

Money down the drain

The next items in your financial feasibility that you need to be aware of are the contributions and charges that different organisations and authorities will levy on you. Quite often, councils will have what's known as an open space contribution, which supposedly is to maintain parks and open spaces in the area. It is often jokingly referred to as the council Christmas party fund.

Usually, the open space contribution is a percentage based on some kind of value, generally the land value and they all have different ways of working that out.

You just need to talk to your local council where you plan to develop to find out how they come up with that figure. It might be five percent of the land value. Quite often duplex projects don't attract an open space contribution, but it varies from council to council. You need to be aware that you might need to pay an open space contribution fee.

The other one is stormwater discharge fees. Whichever organisation looks after the water in the area will charge you a sum of money to access their network. The electricity wholesaler in the area will charge some connection fees to access their network. They may also charge you a fee to build a new pit or some other kind of infrastructure to supply your new homes. Same goes for the gas wholesaler. You also have the NBN Co. for internet and they'll charge you fees to access the NBN network.

They all have different ways of getting their fingers in your pockets. You just need to figure out what those costs are and include them in your feasibility. I go through all these points and more in the Property Developer Training (www.propertydevelopertraining.com) so join up if you want to go through this in more detail.

Next, we're going to be covering construction funding basics because this is probably a topic that fledgling developers are very curious about, as it is such an unknown quantity.

10. Construction funding basics

"You'll do better if you have a passion for something in which you have aptitude.
If Warren Buffet had gone into ballet, no one would have heard of him."
Charlie Munger

What is construction funding? Well, basically, it's the money that you use to pay to build your new units, and it's often quite different to residential investment funding. The banks or lenders will look at it through a completely different lens, so it's very different from residential lending. It's a much shorter loan term and the pricing is very different. That's why it's important that you speak with a specialist broker because there's a bit of dark arts and wizardry that goes on around construction funding.

When lenders look at construction funding applications, they look at it very differently, and they have different people in the bank assessing them. Construction funding is very dynamic and changes all the time. While almost every broker will tell you that they can obtain construction funding, my strong advice is to speak to people who have a lot of experience in this sector and who know how to get you the best possible loan and terms.

Since they tightened their lending standards following the Global Financial Crisis, many mainstream banks have pulled back from providing construction loans. However, many second-tier lenders and non-bank players have moved in to fill the gap. There are now many lenders operating in the market and some of the funding packages can be quite attractive in terms of getting your project off the ground much faster than trying to get the cheapest rate with a bank. This is another conversation to have with your specialist broker.

Acronym soup

Let's have a look at some of the key numbers and terms when you're talking about construction funding. Banks or lenders will start to look more at ratios and percentages when they're looking at your project. Some of the key metrics you need to be aware of are the Total Development Cost (TDC), Gross Realisation Value (GRV), and the amount of equity or cash you have invested in the deal. And, of course, the profit margin.

The amount you can borrow will often be dictated by ratios, and the common ratios are related to the TDC and the GRV. A lender will commonly say something like "we will loan you 80 percent of the TDC or 65 percent of the GRV, whichever is lower". The percentages or ratios the lender will work off will slide around depending on the project, the applicant, funding costs, state of the market, which way the wind is blowing, who's gone to lunch, and anything else they choose to take into consideration!

Here's how that might look, in terms of what you could borrow, based on our working feasibility in chapter nine:

Total Development Cost $1,540,622	80% of TDC $1,232,497	Difference $308,125
Gross Realisation Value $2,095,000	65% of GRV $1,361,750	Difference $178,872

The equity or cash component you would be expected to fund is the difference between the loan and what it will cost to complete the project. In the example above, you can expect the lender to want you to inject at least $308,125 into the project, some of which may be made up from an equity uplift after achieving a permit, which will increase the site value.

There's lots of different ways that lenders try and cut the funding cake to make it work out best for them. For example, with your gross realisation value, they may not take the whole figure into account. They might remove the commission fees and GST before they look at what the GRV figure is. Same applies to the TDC, the lender might exclude the GST amount from the total cost, which will bring down the total amount they will lend you.

Often, lenders won't pay for your GST contributions, so you may have to pull from your own pocket to pay the GST component of any bills that you get from the builder along the way. However, sometimes it is included. I've had GST included in a loan and I've also had it not included. It just differs from lender to lender and project to project.

It's important that you have an experienced construction funding broker to help you for all these reasons and more. You can work closely with them to see how different banks and lenders slice up the cake. A good broker will help you navigate through the lending maze and past the dark wizards that guard the funding vault.

Let's have a look at some of the other key considerations related to construction funding beyond ratios and metrics.

Line fees

This is a charge that gets levied upon you by the lender for the privilege of borrowing money from them. It can get quite costly because it's often charged quarterly, and it will usually be levied on the total amount of money that you're borrowing. That quickly adds up over a period of time, so you need to keep a close eye on it. I have found that line fees can end up being more than interest costs.

The interest rate

Funnily enough, the loan interest rate may not always be the key number you focus on (unlike most residential loans) because you might end up with an effective interest rate that is much higher than the actual interest rate once you factor in all the other fees and costs. Some of the other line fees and application fees might start to add up and may end up increasing the effective interest rate that you pay over the course of the loan.

Application fees

You have the joy of paying for the privilege of actually applying for a construction loan. Usually that will be a percentage of the loan amount that you're seeking. How much you pay depends on the institution/ lender. Banks have fairly low application fees (less than one percent), while private lenders have a higher one (around two percent). It's just a way of them getting more money out of you at the beginning of the project, which reduces their risk.

Let's look at the difference that can make for a million dollar loan.

Bank fee of 0.75 percent = $7,500
Private lender fee of 2 percent = $20,000

One other point to note is that interest will be capitalised on a construction loan (unlike a standard residential loan), so you won't have to pay interest along the way. The interest payments will get capitalised or added to the loan amount along the way and then paid out from settlement funds. When all the new properties settle, your interest payment and any other outstanding loan costs will get settled to retire the construction loan. Capitalising the interest during construction makes a big difference to your cash flow needs.

Debt cover

Lenders will look closely at how much debt they want you to cover. This will be through your cash contribution to the project and also potentially through some pre-sales to further cover off the debt they are going to loan you. Most banks look for 100 percent debt cover from pre-sales, which means if you want to borrow $1 million, they will want to see pre-sales of stock that adds up to $1 million to 'cover' their debt.

The pre-sale debt cover can be challenging to achieve in a soft market. Other lenders or non-banks are less interested in 100 percent debt cover and offer more flexible terms. Private lending is usually assessed much faster, and they're less focused on debt cover. However, it can cost more, so you might be paying a higher interest rate, slightly higher line fee, and you'll certainly be paying a higher application fee. Overall, it might be worth it because you can get construction started sooner rather than waiting around while trying to get some sales.

Those sales may be at a level lower than what you want to get, so you just have to weigh it up. These fees, charges, and costs can really add up over a project, so it is good to get across the likely costs by talking early with a good commercial finance broker. They'll be able to guide you through what's available and how you might be able to get something cheaper and faster or that's more suitable for you.

Applicant strength

When looking at a project that is seeking funding, one area that lenders will look at quite closely is who is applying for the loan and managing the project. They will be very interested in their development history, financial capacity, the financial structure of the project, the type of project and product being delivered, and a whole lot more to determine if the sponsors will be able to actually deliver the project to completion and within budget.

The lender is always considering the worst-case scenario and the likelihood of that happening because they really don't want to step in and have to finish a project or deal with a liquidation. Their specialty is lending money, not delivering property development projects. They want to lend to strong applicants who they believe will safely return their money. This is another area where a great broker can help to present your application in the best possible way.

Dynamic industry

The lending market for construction funding is really dynamic and changing all the time. It's best to stay in touch with a good commercial broker who can help you get your construction loan so that they can keep you abreast of what's happening in the market. It does change really quickly, so make sure you stay on top of it.

To wrap up, we've had a quick look at construction funding and how it differs from standard residential funding. We've talked about some of the key ratios and metrics that get looked at. We've talked about how you capitalise your interest payments so you don't need to pay your interest along the way. Instead, it gets added to the bottom line of what you have to pay back to the bank when your loan concludes, which is very helpful for cash flow. We've talked about banks versus private funding and how you'll need to weigh up which one works best for you.

Now you have some insight into how you can calculate your potential construction funding costs. I've only skimmed over these because there is a lot to cover when it comes to construction finance. I have several modules in the Property Developer Training that go through in more detail the topic of finance, feasibilities, and construction funding. If you want to find out more then head over to www.propertydevelopertraining.com and be sure to use the code 'book' to get a discount.

11. How to become a full-time developer and the million dollar milestone

"Having a vision for what you want is not
enough… vision without execution is hallucination."
Thomas Edison

Most people I know who complete their first development project are so excited about it and surprised by the fact it wasn't as complicated and difficult as they imagined that they excitedly begin planning their next project. Many start to think about how they can transition to developing full time. I should know, I was one of them!

But how do you make the jump to full-time property developer? Well, it may not be as difficult as you think. Let's take a look at a potential pathway. Before you get too excited, my advice is to take things slow and basically finish one project before starting to work on multiple projects, so you have an appreciation for everything that needs to be done from start to finish. Learn to walk before you try to run.

Development Management fees

As I've mentioned previously, cash flow, or lack thereof, is one of the challenges you face as a developer. A project mainly has all cash outflow with very little inflow. One of the options available to you to overcome that is to charge the project a fee to manage everything.

This can be a development management (DM) fee or a project management (PM) fee.

The difference is that a development manager would see the project through from start to finish, whereas a project manager might handle a discreet part of the project like managing the construction of the new dwellings. On a smaller project, you are often both the development and project manager! You coordinate everything.

The point is that you can charge the project a fee to manage things. Here's an idea of what you could charge as a development management fee. A DM fee gets treated like all the other reasonable project costs including design, marketing, construction etc. A professional development manager or project management company will usually charge their fee based on a percentage of the build cost, factoring in complexity, length of time, and other project considerations. As a guide, if you were to engage a professional firm to manage your project, you would be looking at:

- 4-5 percent for up to $1 million

- 3-4 percent between $1-5 million

- 2-3 percent between $5-10 million

Remembering that these are professional firms, you will be paying for their expertise, systems, overheads, and profit margin. As part of your project research you could call some of the project management companies that service the area and glean what sort of rates they charge for projects. This will give you a good idea of what the going rate is for professionals to manage the job.

I suggest you look to charge your first couple of projects at a lower rate than the pros, until you can determine what level of value you think, or can demonstrate, that you bring to the table. If you are running a project with a million dollar construction cost, you could potentially charge two to three percent as you get started, so $20,000 to $30,000 to manage the whole thing. Remembering, on average you will be spending 10-14 hours a week running a project. Some weeks will be more, some weeks will be less.

Learning on the job

On your first project, you probably won't charge a fee because you understand that you are learning on the job and want to get a feel for what's involved. The fee for your time will be wrapped up in the profit the project makes. But there's nothing stopping you from factoring a management fee into your first project's feasibility and collecting payment for all the work you do.

The fee you charge is not set in stone and can change from project to project but it gives you an idea of what you could reasonably factor into a feasibility to compensate you for all the time, effort, and sweat that you put into successfully completing a project. Over time you will refine this fee based on your experience and the expected complexity of a project.

If you can consistently work on two or three projects a year, you could potentially earn more than $60,000 to $90,000 a year in fees, and that's before we start talking about profits. Now, you are going to be busy running those projects. It won't be money for jam. You will be juggling a team of people. You will be working on solving problems. You will be making a lot of decisions. You will be conducting the orchestra. But chances are that you will be enjoying it.

Charging for legitimate project costs

Another way that you can extract cash from a project is through providing legitimate services or deliverables. For example, you may be a qualified accountant and you can manage the project's books and spend 12 hours a quarter ensuring the accounts are all squared away. This work has to be done and is a legitimate project cost. Somebody would have to be paid to do this work anyway, so if you are qualified to do that then you could potentially charge a fair and reasonable fee to the project for the work.

Here's a working example, I have video production skills and during projects I often produce videos for sales campaigns instead of outsourcing it to a video production company. I spend time producing those videos so I will charge the project a reasonable amount for delivering them. It is a cost that would have been incurred by the project anyway. If I provide the service and deliver something of acceptable quality, the money goes to me rather than an external consultant.

This is not an excuse for you to start charging the project all sorts of wild fees above any management fees. If you are not a graphic designer, punching out some 'marketing collateral' using PowerPoint and issuing the project a massive invoice is not going to cut it as a legitimate or reasonable service.

Working for #1

Wouldn't you rather be busy working for yourself and generating your own wealth as opposed to working for 'the man'? "Hell yeah!" I hear you say! I can tell you that since I left my job as an employee, I haven't really felt as if I have been working. It feels different when you are working on your own projects and towards your own goals. It comes with responsibilities and obligations, it's not a hobby anymore. For me it is worth it and deeply fulfilling.

Which reminds me of a seminal moment in my life when I was working for 'the man' and I was seeking a promotion. My manager was supportive and suggested I put my case forward for a raise. I was told to write a memo to the big boss outlining why I felt I should be promoted. I set to work and crafted a bureaucratic memorandum of sheer beauty. Laying out, piece, by compelling piece, why I should take one step up the corporate ladder. I refined it and polished it until it was gleaming. I then sent it up the line, hopeful that my wish would be granted.

Surely, I was worth the extra money. I demonstrated it magnificently in the memo. So, what do you think happened? That's right, it got knocked back. I remember riding (I used to commute on bicycle) home from work the day I found out, frustrated and disappointed that my financial situation was being controlled by the corporate overlords. It also was a timely reminder that if I didn't want to be subject to other people deciding what I could earn, then I had to take my financial destiny into my own hands.

Raising the stakes

I know what you are wondering, how much was the raise I was seeking? A measly $1,500. A $28 weekly increase. To this day, I still remember this event so clearly because now if I want to make an extra $1,500, I can negotiate that off a quote or look at ways to save that somewhere in a project.

I'm no longer worried about $1,500 raises, as I have far more control over how I make extra money and it is usually more than $1,500. It was a great lesson, and it has served me well. That's the risk and life of working in a corporate machine, it is never really about you, and you play by their rules.

Anyway, management fees are part of the plan toward becoming a million-dollar property developer. They provide some cash flow and interim reward between the profit events. Your earning potential now comes down to how many projects you can pull together and effectively manage.

Beat the average

When I am writing this, the average income in Australia is around $65,000. Before tax. Sure, there are people in major cities earning far more than that, but it gets eaten up in living costs. For the 'average' employee in Australia to 'earn' a million dollars they would have to work for 15 years. Then there's taxes, living costs, lifestyle expenses, etc. How long do you think it would take the average person to 'bank' a million or create equity of a million? Most will never get close.

You don't have to wait that long to earn a million, I've just shown you how you can 'earn' more than the 'average' person in one year, doing something you enjoy. Three projects a year is very manageable if you are doing it full time. Or you could manage the project on the side while you continue whatever job you hold down and pocket an additional $20,000 to $30,000 each year or two, on top of the profit pay-out at the end. You can slowly build your skills and experience up and plan your exit, if that's what you want. It won't be long until you start thinking of scaling or going to bigger projects, maybe both.

The point I am trying to make is that you can be passive, sit, wait, and hope for that million to come your way in the next decade or more. Or, you can be active, inspired, and in control of manufacturing that million in the next five, six, or seven years. How quick you do this is up to you. I am showing you how it is closer than you probably think.

Profitability

Let's get down to business. How can you become a million-dollar property developer? What sort of profits can you expect from projects? Well, the answer is it depends. There used to be a magic figure of having a 15 percent profit margin that was thrown around for small to medium sized projects as a profitability benchmark because banks wanted to see that kind of margin on a project before they would provide construction funding. A 15 percent margin allows for a lot of stuff ups before the bank starts risking its money on a project that doesn't go to plan.

An acceptable margin really depends on the deal and the person running the project. For a quick and simple project with very low risk, you might be happy with a seven percent return. But a larger, more complicated 20-townhouse project, for example, would certainly be looking to get well above a 15 percent return. You might decide that a 10 percent return on a straightforward duplex project that takes 12 months is pretty good for the money and time you put in.

However, obtaining funding may be dependent on the projected margin to be achieved, along with a range of other factors, so it would be prudent to discuss this with your broker.

Remember that margins don't put food on the table, absolute returns do. The $100,000 profit that goes into your bank account from the simple duplex project can be a great reward for the risk (low) and your effort (minimal), especially when coupled with your management fee. You can look at it like this, you are getting paid to manufacture assets and grow your own wealth. Sounds good to me!

Pathway to $100,000 a year and a million dollars

Let's take a look at a possible pathway to earning $100,000 a year within three years and generating $1 million in wealth in five years. Here's an example of how you could make it happen.

This is a pathway based on conservative results on a small three- or four-unit project.

Please remember that these are general numbers, every project and location will have different results, but you can see how you can grow your fees, profits, and wealth.

There are a few assumptions here. The numbers are gross figures. Profits increase over time; this may be due to you becoming smarter and more efficient or negotiating better deals. Your management fees increase over time as you become more adept and professional at delivering profitable projects. You begin taking on multiple projects a year to boost your profits and fees.

There is also an assumption that you stop doing any projects from year six, for the purpose of illustration. You can see that generating a cumulative wealth of $1,000,000 in five years is achievable.

Year	Fees	Profit	Annual Revenue	Cumulative
1 - start project 1	$20,000	$0	$20,000	$20,000
2 - start project 2	$20,000	$0	$20,000	$40,000
3 - start project 3 and 4 Profit from Project 1	$50,000 (bumped up fees by $5,000 a project due to experience so $25,000 a project)	$175,000	$225,000	$265,000
4 - start projects 4, 5 and 6 Profit from project 2	$75,000	$200,000	$275,000	$540,000
5 - start projects 7, 8 and 9 Profits from projects 3 and 4	$90,000 (bumped up fees by $5,000 due to experience so $30,000 a project)	$400,000	$490,000	$1,030,000

6 - Profits from projects 4, 5 and 6		$675,000	$675,000	$1,705,000
7 - Profits from projects 7, 8 and 9		$675,000	$675,000	$2,380,000
	$255,000	$2,125,000		

This model could be accelerated by taking on bigger projects, doing more projects, or a combination of both. The beauty of property development is that your earnings potential is capped only by your desire for success, and how much effort and work you want to put in toward your future and growing wealth.

How does this model compare to the next five years of the job or career you are currently in?

12. What type of person makes a good property developer?

"We are what we repeatedly do. Excellence then is not an act, but a habit."
Aristotle

Let's talk about the kinds of people that I think make good property developers because there's all sorts of different people that are doing developments. It ranges from people doing simple duplex projects to others doing three- or four-unit projects. Then you have people taking on high rise developments and big land subdivisions. You see all kinds of people working to deliver a project.

Here's a couple of traits that I think would serve you well in property development.

1. You're flexible

I've mentioned many times that there's a lot of things that happen in a property development project. There are a lot of decisions to be made, reports that need to be produced, and questions that get asked. There are a lot of changes that need to be made, so you need to be flexible and adaptable to what gets thrown your way. There will be problems. There are going to be challenges, but you need to work with your team to come up with the solutions. More often than not, there is a solution, it just depends on how you get there. It might involve spending money or experiencing a delay. The worst is when it costs time and money! Whatever it is, you just need to remain flexible and nimble, find the solution, make the decision, and move on.

2. Resilience

The second character trait that I think is helpful in property development is being resilient. You don't let setbacks stop you from moving ahead, because there are going to be hurdles and roadblocks. Things that come up along the way that are going to challenge you. You will need to overcome them, just like anything in life. If it was easy, everybody would do it. You need to be resilient because you're going to get challenged, you're going to face obstacles, and you need to overcome them and move on.

3. Work well with others

The third trait that I think is helpful if you want to get into property development is working well with lots of different people. In the end, property development is a relationship game. You're dealing with humans at every step of the way. You're going to be working with designers, real estate agents, engineers, buyers, council staff, all sorts of different people. If you struggle doing that, then I think you're really going to struggle in property development. Which is not to say that you need to be super friendly and everybody's bestie, but you need to be able to work constructively with a variety of people.

4. Able to delegate

The fourth trait I think is helpful in property development is the ability to delegate. You simply cannot do everything on your own. In property development, you need a big team. You can't draw the design of your new dwellings. You can't write the town planning report to go with your application. You can't prepare the funding application. You can't sell all the properties. You're going to need help along the way, and you need to delegate. If you have trouble delegating and letting go and having other people do things for you, you're really going to struggle being a property developer.

5. Problem solver

The fifth trait of good property developers is people who enjoy solving problems and working out solutions. That doesn't mean you need to come up with the solutions to all the problems. You simply cannot because there's too many technical issues to be across, but you need to be good at working with people to come up with those solutions.

You will have people present you with options so that you can make a decision, and sometimes you won't have all the information available to you. You will have to make the best decision that you can with the information provided to you at that point in time. However, that's not unusual in business. It's more unusual to have all the information available to you when you need to decide something.

If you do enjoy solving problems, then property development may be a rewarding experience because there are lots of problems that need to be solved along the way.

6. Have a purpose

The next trait that I think is super important for a property developer is somebody who is purposeful. If you have a great reason for getting into property development and delivering projects, a strong reason for succeeding, then I think you'll do well in property development.

That purpose is going to drive you through all the challenges and obstacles that you're going to face. If you've got a deep enough reason why you are doing property development, that's going to be really helpful. It might be that you want to create a better lifestyle for your family, send the kids to better schools or through university. Whatever it is, it will make a difference to understand your purpose when the going gets tough.

7. Frugalist

The final trait that I think is helpful in property development is people who are frugal. Now that's not to be confused with people who are cheap, but more people who are really good at keeping a tight rein on spending. They keep a good eye on expenses and how much things cost. They ask for discounts off fees and proposals. They see where they can obtain extra value for no extra cost. Now I will often say, don't go for the cheapest option, go for the best value option, and I think that's what frugal people do. They're not looking for the cheapest. They're looking for the best value. So, if you're good at being frugal, then that is a good trait for being a property developer.

There you go, those are some of the traits that I think make for a good property developer. If you would like to find out how ready you might be to become a property developer, take my free quiz at: www.propertydevelopertraining.com/quiz

13. The traits of people who might struggle with property development

"To get what you love, you must first be patient with what you hate."
Al-Ghazali

We've been through some of the key traits of successful property developers, so let's now go through the types of people who I think would struggle with property development. I think there's a couple of traits or personality characteristics that aren't the best suited for the property development game. So, who do I think would struggle?

1.   Perfectionists

First, I think perfectionists might struggle with the changes and compromises that need to be made during a project. I'm sure there's a place for perfectionists in property development, but in my experience, you need to be flexible and adaptable, so you are ready to make changes along the way. So many challenging things pop up, like people asking for changes to be made. I think if you were really focused on perfection that you might struggle to cope with all the changes that happen throughout a project. I like the saying production, not perfection, and I think that applies to property development. You really need to keep pushing things along.

2.   Quitters

The second characteristic of people who might struggle are quitters. People with little to no resilience, who will wilt under any kind of pressure. You need to be able to resist some of that pressure or you won't be able to push through. You don't need to be SAS-level resilient and able to stand in the snow for 24 hours with no food or water, but you need to be able to take a few knocks or glancing blows and not let it get you down.

As I just mentioned, you are going to have challenges along the way. You are going to have unexpected issues pop up, and you just need to be ready to deal with them. People who quit easily or fold easily are not really suitable for property development.

If you're going to curl up and cry on the couch every time something doesn't go your way, you're going to be spending a lot of time on the couch crying. That's not to say that occasionally you might crawl into bed and have a big fat cry because something dramatic has happened. You can do that, have a little or big cry, and let it all out. However, you need to pull yourself together quickly and then get on with the job of solving whatever problem is in your way. Property development is not for quitters.

3.   Tyrants

The third type of person that I don't think is suitable for property development is tyrants. Property development is a team game. Yes, you are the lone conductor of the orchestra, but you're also the captain of the team, and you need a lot of people to help you. All those people are humans. They're all different, so you can't yell and scream and expect to create a great team.

It's not common for people to enjoy being yelled at and blamed. If that's your standard mode of operation, then I think you're going to struggle to build a great team or to continue working with good people. Quality people, effective consultants, and other good team members are not going to stick around and work with someone they don't like.

Which is not to say that you can let people get away with anything, but I find that you get more discretionary effort from people if you can be polite, proactive, and constructive. It's amazing what you can get done by asking quality questions rather than demanding things. As Abraham Lincoln once famously said, "it's easier to catch a bunch of flies with an ounce of honey than a gallon of gall".

There might be times when you need to be tough and have difficult conversations when something goes wrong but I don't think that you need to resort to yelling and screaming at people. You may need to take charge, be assertive and ensure that things get done on time and to a high-quality standard. However, I think there's a big difference between being a tyrant and being a leader.

4.   Pushovers

The fourth type of people who I don't think are suitable for property development are the pushovers. These are the kind of people who believe everything they hear or read and accept everything they're told. You get told 'no' a lot during a project. From consultants, councils, authorities, anybody who has a say in something and sometimes it's not a real 'no'. It's more an easy 'no'.

You have to unpick the 'no' and figure out if there is a way around it. It might be more expensive, or it might take a little bit longer but there is often a way. You just need to work out what it is. You can't just accept no for an answer. I've certainly pushed back on lots of 'no's' from councils and other people and found a way to work around the objection that they've raised. I have not always succeeded in getting around things but often enough there is usually a solution if you keep digging. You can't be a pushover if you plan on succeeding in property development.

5.   Hotheads

The fifth character trait or type of person who I think would struggle in property development are the hotheads. These are the people who blow up easily when things go awry, and they blame everybody else. Nobody really likes working with a hothead. There are just so many things that happen throughout a property development project. Some of them are unexpected, and if you're going to be cracking it every time something doesn't go according to plan, you're going to be spending a lot of time upset. As I mentioned previously, good people are not going to want to work with hotheads for very long. You need to try and stay calm and work your way through the problem.

If you're a hot head and you like to blame other people, then I don't think property development is going to be right for you. This leads on to the next character trait that I think is problematic for people who want to get into development.

6.   Overly emotive

People who are overly emotive will have a tough time during a project because property development can be a real roller coaster. Funny things pop up. There are unexpected challenges that cost time and money. You need to try and keep a level head to make good, prompt decisions. If you're going to get really upset about all the things that happen along the way, you're going to spend a lot of time upset. You need to try to maintain some equanimity and some balance in perspective. Look at your options, look at the challenges and then make a decision to move forward.

7.   Easyriders

The next type of people who I think wouldn't do very well in property development are the easyriders. The get rich quick merchants who are looking for easy money. The people who think it's just straightforward to succeed in property development. You buy a block of land, get a planning permit, build the new units, sell them for a million bucks, and bank the profit.

It doesn't quite work that way. Yes, you can make good money from property development and really leverage your time, but it's a get rich quicker program, not a get rich quick scheme. It still takes time to build up the capital base and grow your assets.

If you're looking for the quick, easy millions, I think you should be looking elsewhere.

8.   Desperados

The next type of people who are not ideal for property development are the desperados. If you're really desperate to make easy millions, then I think you're going to come unstuck in property development because desperation leads to making poor decisions. You need to make quality, well thought through decisions. You should gather as much information together as you can to make an informed decision. You don't want to operate in a desperate way. You want to be balanced and stable when making decisions. Being desperate is not to be confused with people who are determined to succeed. I think being determined is a good thing. Perhaps being desperate to succeed could be a good thing, but you don't want that desperation to poorly affect your decision making.

9.   Rigidity

The next type of character trait that doesn't lend itself too well to property developing is people who are too rigid. This extends from what we were talking about with the perfectionists. There are just so many things that happen in a project. So many decisions to be made, unexpected hurdles that pop up, and you need to be able to bend and flex and adapt to whatever situation you are in.

If you're too rigid, if you're just going to stick to whatever your plan was or whatever your idea was, well, you might find that you hit a dead end or you come up against fierce resistance from, say, a council who doesn't agree with how many units you want to do.

There are so many things that could trip you up if you're really rigid and you just want to stick with your idea. I found this out the hard way on my second project when I stuck to my guns with the number of units that I wanted to have in my project. I was convinced that 19 units would be acceptable and supported at the planning tribunal. All the consultants on my team agreed with me. The council planners said that they would accept 17, but I stuck to 19 and when we got the decision from the tribunal, we ended up losing. This is a really good example about being too rigid. It also shows the risk of confirmation bias, when people tell you what you want to hear.

In hindsight, I think if we had adapted our scheme and gone with a 17-townhouse proposal, I think we would have had a much better chance of winning. I think we may have actually scraped across the line. I was too rigid and paid a heavy price. So let that be a lesson to you to remain flexible and not be too rigid.

10. Hand holders

The other type of people who may struggle with property development are people who like to have somebody reassure them that the decisions they make are correct. Ultimately, you have to make decisions and be accountable for them. If you need someone to hold your hand and always reassure you that what you're doing is the right thing, I think you're going to struggle to lead a team and get the project done. At some point you're going to have to make decisions.

Sometimes you have to make a decision without knowing all the information you'd like to know, but you just have to make the best decision that you can. If you'd like to have people reassuring you all the time, property development may not be your game.

It can also be somewhat of a lonely game. It can just be you, in the end, having to make a decision about what to do. No one really understands the full picture of the project except for you. If you can't handle that, you might struggle.

11. Fantasists

The final and perhaps most important group who may struggle with property development are the fantasists. The people who think that property development is easy money. They've got the fantasy about driving the fast car, the Lamborghini, the Ferrari. They want to enjoy the lifestyle of flying first class and living in big houses, since they think it's all going to come really easily. They don't really need to do anything. They just buy the land, get the planning permit, build the houses, sell them for squillions, and off they go.

What happens is people find out it's not that straightforward. It can be quite challenging to find a profitable development site. You have to work hard to find it and to secure it. Those people are not really ready to work for their millions.

They want the easy outcome, and very rarely does property development provide the easy outcome. It does provide good rewards if you get in there and work hard for it, but you need to do the work.

That's a brief summary of the character traits of the kind of people who I think would struggle with property development.

If you would like to find out how ready you might be to become a property developer, take my free quiz at www.propertydevelopertraining.com/quiz

14. Common Traps and Pitfalls to Avoid

"To accept something on mere presumption and, likewise, to fail to investigate it may cover over, blind and lead astray."
Al-Farabi

Time to talk about common traps and pitfalls that fledgling developers can fall into. Let's cover 13 common pitfalls that I've seen and experienced in my time doing property development. I'll also explain why they can really hurt.

1. Think it will be easy

The first trap or pitfall to avoid is thinking that property development is going to be easy. Property development isn't necessarily hard, but it's also not easy because unexpected things pop up. People make mistakes, including you. Councils are going to ask for crazy things. Weird stuff is going to happen.

If you are potentially going to make hundreds of thousands of dollars in profit, or maybe even millions, do you really think it's going to be easy? It pays to understand that you just need to solve whatever problem comes up. It usually involves time or money. Hopefully not both! In the end, all property development requires is the ability to problem solve and work with lots of different people.

So, be prepared for the issues that are going to pop up and work with your team to solve them. I go back to how important it is to have a purpose for doing a project and for doing development, because it's helpful as a reason to drive you forward when the going gets tough. The universe isn't designed to give away riches easily. The people that can solve problems get paid and the bigger the problems you can solve, the bigger the pay-out you can expect. Don't expect it to be easy and be ready for the challenges.

2.   Getting thrown off by setbacks

The second trap or pitfall that people fall into is letting setbacks stump them. As I've just mentioned, part of the game is dealing with challenges and issues that pop up along the way. I suggest that it's a good idea just to embrace those challenges, focus on the problem, work out how to solve it, learn and move on. It's too easy to curl up on the couch and cry when the going gets tough.

I remember during my first project; I was shocked that the build quote came in about $400,000 more than I expected. I spent months trying to find cost saving measures and driving the costs down. I spent a lot of time looking backwards instead of looking forwards to keep the project moving. Fortunately for me, the market went up and the extra cost from the time lost was covered by the price rises. But usually time costs money, and the longer you take, the less profit you make. Thus, when you're faced with a problem, get to work and find the best solution.

3.   Manipulating the feasibility

The third issue to try and avoid is manipulating the feasibility. It's really easy to adjust and tweak numbers in the feaso to achieve a 15 percent return or whatever kind of return you're looking for. It's easy to boost the sales figures by $10,000 each. It's easy to reduce the build costs by $10,000 and boom! The project works on paper but do this at your own risk.

I would encourage you to be realistic with your numbers. You should not be conservative or overly optimistic, but realistic. I know it can get frustrating when you're looking at heaps and heaps of sites, and nothing seems to be working. You want to start making something fit into your expectations, and you start to tweak and push and pull the feaso to make something work. But the only person that you're going to be tricking by doing that is yourself. Be wary of doing it.

4.   Wrong people helping you

Having the wrong team members or sticking with the wrong people can be really costly, and can slow turnaround times. You need to make sure that you've got the right people on your team to help you along the way. I once used a draftsperson that was not particularly good at being accountable for things. I had a sense that they weren't acting as quickly as they could and weren't really the right fit for my project. It probably cost me six to nine months in delays until I figured out that this person really wasn't the right person to have on the team.

In retrospect, I would have been better off by moving to another designer months before I did. It's a good idea to have really good people around you who are supportive and competent to help you get things done as quickly as possible.

5.   Not having enough cash

The next one is a really big one. It's about not having enough cash to complete your project. That's how developers go into liquidation and come unstuck. All because they just don't have the cash to pay to get things finished. I think it's better to be liquid and fully funded. So, work hard to ensure that you've got sufficient funds at each stage of a project.

What I have found is that unexpected things come up. Some invoices end up being higher than you expected. There will be delays that add additional costs. If you're scrounging around, trying to pay for all those things it becomes really tiring and stressful. Try and have enough cash and contingency funds to get you through without having to sell your stamp collection or furniture or whatever it is that you need to liquidate to finish the project.

6. Poor due diligence

The next trap and pitfall to avoid is conducting poor due diligence on a project. Due diligence is the work you do to determine if a site is suitable or not. I hope that by going through my Property Developer Training, you don't fall into this trap. Many people get caught out by not doing enough due diligence which makes them not discover an obvious or identifiable issue before buying the site. Solid due diligence on a site goes a long way toward ensuring the overall success of your project. It means you can buy a site with confidence.

7. Paying too much for a site

There's a saying in property that the profits are made in the buying, which is often very true. It's hard to come back from paying too much for a site. There's a lot of flow-on effects that will impact you as the project goes on. It will be hard to get funding. It will be a real drain on your energy because who wants to end up working for a couple of years for nothing? Not me, that's for sure.

It's really easy to get excited and emotional about a project. You might want to go all in at almost any cost. But beware of the consequences. You don't want to be waiting seven years to develop a site that you thought was going to take two. You may need to hold onto it and wait for the market to move. This is especially important to consider if the market is frenzied and many buyers eagerly jump in and overpay for properties. How much over market value you might pay depends on the project size and the location. Paying five percent more for a site could potentially harm your profit prospects and lead to a couple of years of really hard slog and stress. Be prudent in what you pay for a site.

8. Being passive instead of active

Pitfall number eight is being passive instead of active. It's really easy to wait around for things to happen instead of making them happen. That is a recipe for trouble in property development. Action creates reaction, and we always want to see action. For example, it's easy to let a consultant say that it will be a few weeks until you get your report. But how long is a few weeks? Is it one week? Is it two weeks? It's better to ask for a firm date so that you can hold people accountable. Allowing things to drift along will have knock-on effects throughout the project. So, keep pushing things along and don't let things drift.

9. Believing people who say 'no'

Trap number nine is believing people who say 'no'. Now this is very, very common for a whole range of reasons. Many people like to project the worst outcome, or they don't like change, or they enjoy saying 'no'.

There are going to be many people who will say no to you, including your friends and family, objectors who live around your site, lenders, councils, the list is endless. However, don't believe it to be true. It's not always the case that something can't be done. I suggest that you make your own decisions. Follow your own dreams and focus on your purpose and keep investigating something until you are fully satisfied that it can't be done. Maybe you just need to make a change or do something a little differently, but it doesn't mean you can't do it, so don't just easily accept 'no!'

10. Having hard conversations when they are needed

Number 10 is being prepared to have the hard conversations when they are needed. It can be really challenging to call out mistakes that get made by the builder or by someone on your team. Flaws in design or delays can be really costly and challenging the council about why they ask for something that you think is unreasonable is a pain. That's your role as the project director.

It's really important to have those discussions. You need to air your concerns and get solutions. It's really a disservice to the project and to yourself if you let things slide that need to be addressed. Property development is not a popularity contest, but it is a competency contest. Always look to be competent. If you need to have a tough conversation, then just do it.

11. Being a cheapskate

Next on my list of traps and pitfalls to avoid is being a cheapskate. This means always looking for the lowest price and should not be confused with being frugal. It's tempting to automatically go for the cheapest builder or the cheapest consultant, but maybe it's going to be more costly in the long run.

If the builder goes bust or stuffs up, you're going to be in a really sticky situation because it's going to take months and months to sort something out. If you get a poor plan prepared by somebody, it could take weeks, potentially months, to get that sorted out. Sure, be mindful of cost and always seek efficiency, but not at the cost of value.

Seek out people who are experienced and competent. Be prepared to pay for good advice. What's the worst thing about paying for good advice? You pay a little bit more. The worst thing that can happen from poor advice or work is always a lot more costly and stressful. That doesn't mean that you can't ask for discounts or ways of adding additional value to a quote, just be value driven. Always.

12. Not reviewing things

The next item on my list of traps and pitfalls to avoid is not reviewing things that get done for you. I can't begin to tell you the number of reports or work that has been done for me that I have checked or reviewed only to find glaring omissions or mistakes. Things that I've asked to be fixed haven't been fixed or things to be changed haven't been changed or issues haven't been addressed.

This is obviously easier if it's a written report, because you can read it. But if it's technical drawings, that gets a bit more complicated. However, you can still get people to check them on your behalf. You really need to read through the reports that people prepare for you so that you know what they're actually writing or preparing on your behalf.

This also applies to checking and confirming whether things have actually been done. Did the council receive the planning submission? Did the solicitor receive the deposit funds from the purchaser? Did the agent send the information you provided to the buyer? It is surprising how often you find out that something important that claims to be done, hasn't in fact been done.

As explained in a previous chapter, I once had a request for a time extension on a planning application submitted late and the council tried to cancel the application. I had to spend a lot of time and effort resolving that massive spot fire. It could have been avoided if I had ensured the extension request was actioned earlier by the person acting on my behalf.

I think it's really, really important that you review things being done on your behalf. Coupled with that is the need to be prepared to challenge and ask questions of people that do work for you. Ask them to explain something in a report. If you don't understand what it means, then challenge them. If you don't think it addresses the issue that they've been asked to fix, then raise it.

In my experience, it is so worthwhile reading through and finding out what people are writing. You will be amazed at the things that you pick up that you think aren't quite right. You will also gain knowledge about the topic covered. Always be sure to review everything that gets done for you.

13. Thinking the market will stay the same or improve

The property market is dynamic. It is always changing. Day to day, week to week. It is very hard to predict exactly where it is going to be in 12 months, two years, five years, or 10 years. Historically, the Australian property market has trended up and I think that will continue for the next 25 years, with some ups and downs along the way. A challenge for developers is predicting exactly where the market will be in 12 months in terms of new property prices. People can become unstuck if they rely on prices to improve to make their feasibility work. If the market stagnates or goes backwards, they end up in big trouble. I have seen it happen.

You buy at the top of a market with prices quite high to secure the site. To make it work, you add five percent to the end sales prices figuring that's where prices are heading and where they will remain when you start selling off the plan. But something happens like a regulation change or an unexpected economic setback that ripples through the market, and suddenly the end sale prices are not five percent higher, but instead five percent lower. That's a big swing. You can't sell the site for enough to make back all your costs, and you can't develop the site because you won't make any money. You are stuck.

It would be wiser to have considered this outcome and have a plan to deal with it. Like we discussed in the fear and risk section. If we had considered this scenario, we would have a plan for it. Maybe we hold on to the site, rent it out longer, and wait for the market to shift again. Which, it eventually will. The point is to consider what might happen and plan for it. The market is going to change, we can be sure of that. Whether it is up or down is out of our control, but having a plan is within our control.

There are certainly many traps and pitfalls in property development. It is one of the reasons that people get scared off. But if you are aware of them, stay focused on how to avoid them and with good people supporting you, you can sidestep the big, fat problems that can bring people unstuck.

15. What does an amazing life look like?

"Let no act be done without purpose."
Marcus Aurelius

Have you ever given much thought to what your most amazing life might look like? I'm sure you have fantasised and day-dreamed about it. Nice cars, beautiful houses, foreign holidays, more time doing the things you enjoy… we each have a different fantastical life. What are you doing to make it become a reality?

I write this because I believe that you can achieve that lifestyle if it is what you really want. I often say that having a clear purpose for why you are getting into property development is very important because it will help you overcome the hurdles and obstacles along the way. If you are working toward a goal or lifestyle that is genuinely important to you, it will inspire you to forge ahead.

Now, I'm talking about a life that is truly meaningful and fulfilling to you, not a fantasy. Do you really want to lie by a pool all day every day? It might be fun for a week or two, but every day for a year? I suspect you'd get bored after a while.

Anyway, whatever you think you want to have in your life, start writing it down. Look at it every day. Add to it. Refine it. Refer to it. Use it as fuel to fire your energy and inspire you to bigger and better things. It will help you get through those challenging moments, the low points. The problems that seem intractable.

The hurdle that seems too high.

Funny things happen when you keep chipping away at your goals, even the biggest ones. Over time, they start to come true. I love the saying that you don't need to be great to get started, but you need to start to be great.

So, what does your amazing life look like?

What would truly make you feel fulfilled?

If you could do anything without fear of failing, what would it be?

Start writing it down and go after it.

16. Wrapping up

"Don't be pushed by your problems. Be led by your dreams."
Ralph Waldo Emerson

My purpose in writing this book was to open your awareness to the possibilities that property developing could bring to your life. If you have toyed with the idea of getting into property development, I hope this book has given you some insight into what skills, traits, and approaches tend to work well throughout a project.

I covered my bizarre journey from public servant to property developer, sharing with you some of the ups and downs I have experienced along the way. Starting out with a 20-townhouse project as my first development, then moving on to a 14-unit development. That one involved a failed trip to the planning tribunal. After that, I took on another 14-unit project right next door to my first project.

Along the way, I established my own podcast dedicated to property development, the first regular podcast about property development in the world. I did it to help share the stories of developers and people involved with the industry, to inspire others, and help people take their developing business to the next level. If you haven't already, I invite you to tune in at www.propertydeveloperpodcast.com for all the great conversations I have with people.

Following on from the success of the podcast and all the emails I received from aspiring developers, I created the Property Developer Training. It's an online course that takes you step by step through the property development process. You can take the course in your own time, at your own pace, and it is designed for those entry level projects like duplexes or three/four-unit sites.

I have taken all the hard-won lessons from my mistakes and successes and rolled them all into the training. If that sounds like it might be of interest to you, head over to www.propertydevelopertraining.com and use the code 'book' to get a deep discount.

I have given you a high-level overview of a financial feasibility and been through some construction funding basics to give you an idea of what is needed to determine if a project is viable.

If this book inspires you to take a step toward getting started in property development, then I will be delighted and thrilled for you. If you would like to see how ready you are to become a property developer, then take the free quiz at www.propertydevelopertraining. com/quiz

I have shown you that generating a million dollars from property development could be achieved in five years without a great deal of risk, provided you know what you are doing, and you put in the work. Developing is not a hit and hope endeavour.

Life is what you make of it. Nobody is going to wake up in the morning dedicated to making your life better, so you need to do that yourself. You could be the next million-dollar property developer in Australia. Heck, you could be the next billion-dollar property developer, it's up to you. The opportunity exists. Wealth, fulfilment, and glory awaits.

I wish you all the best on your journey. See you at the top.

Yours in developing

Justin

About the author

Justin Gehde is the director of Melbourne-based property developer GEHDE, which has a strong track record of delivering medium-sized townhouse projects.

Justin has led development projects worth more than $24 million dollars, and at the time of publishing, has built or is building nearly 50 townhouses.

He is responsible for all elements of a development project from sourcing and securing sites and managing the planning application through to sales and coordinating construction.

Justin is the host of the Property Developer Podcast, where he discusses all things property development with a range of industry players. You can find the podcast at www.propertydeveloperpodcast.com

Prior to becoming a full-time property developer, Justin worked in corporate roles for nearly 20 years before escaping the cubicle and building the life of his dreams.

Justin has a Bachelor of Business and an Associate Diploma in Business Management. He is married with two children (and two cats).

You can find Justin in the following places:

Instagram: https://www.instagram.com/property_developer_podcast/

LinkedIn: https://www.linkedin.com/company/property-developer-podcast

Facebook: https://www.facebook.com/propertydeveloperpodcast